EXIT THE SPIRAL

A CALL TO CLASSIC SANITY
IN A PROGRESSIVELY MISGUIDED WORLD

THADDEUS KUNTZ

Copyright © 2019 by Thaddeus Kuntz

Printed in the United States of America

ISBN 978-0-9853134-0-1 (Softcover)

All rights reserved.

TO SOULS

CONTENTS

CHAPTER SUMMARIES	vii
ACKNOWLEDGMENTS	ix
PREFACE	xi
INTRODUCTION	1
1. REASONABLE PROOF	
Limits	7
Expectations	11
Conclusions	21
2. MORAL TAPROOTS	
Irresponsibility	33
Negligence	47
Disrespect	57
Selfishness	67
Pride	74
3. VITAL FAITH	
Cognition	89
Vision	97
Educability	111
4. POTENT APPEARANCE	
Weight	123
Plasticity	130
5. THE SETTING	
Jurisdiction	145
Implication	162
Relevance	179
APPENDIX	186
SUGGESTED ANSWERS	195
NOTES	211
INDEX	226

CHAPTER SUMMARIES

1. REASONABLE PROOF

    Public institutions have taught philosophy-based speculations as fact. This chapter briefly addresses the concept of and need for valid conclusions and the fundamental flaws of certain entrenched assumptions.

2. MORAL TAPROOTS

    Modernistic philosophy is attacking and reversing the morality of the American people. This chapter explores the grim end and misleading nature of progressive rationale and reveals the diverse benefits and native honesty of traditional morals.

3. VITAL FAITH

    Secular humanism works hard to downplay the role of faith in our lives. This chapter reveals the absolute necessity of faith in our everyday lives and the irrationality of denying its importance.

4. POTENT APPEARANCE

    Pervasive media leverages images with surprising and hellish success. This chapter probes into the essential meaning of images, both their importance and their volatility.

5. THE SETTING

    Rational discussion must conform to the finite boundaries of nature. This final chapter unveils some of the beauty and beneficial restriction inherent in the physical realm.

ACKNOWLEDGMENTS

The development of this resource benefited greatly from the generous insights and diligent efforts of several individuals. Long before the theme of this book came to mind, the vision and selfless devotion of my parents inspired a personal passion for life and a thirst for truth. Their godly faith shone most brightly after the loss of my youngest sister, Cassia, and through the disabilities of my closest brother, Jacob. In spite of these and many other challenges, my parents were always faithful to a local church.

As a teenager, I was influenced profoundly by the life and faith of Pastor Kevin Leary. On many occasions Pastor Kevin took time to answer my questions and listen to my concerns. While our ways have separated with time, his guidance in those deciding years will forever remain outstanding in my hindsight.

As an adult, I have received invaluable counsel from Dr. David Costantino. He directed me to Grace Baptist College, where I finished my degrees and was honored to learn under Dr. Jon Jenkins. Pastor Costantino has been quick to answer my questions and patient with my misunderstandings and concerns; he has steered me safely through some stormy waters, and I will be forever indebted to his wise leadership.

Mr. Dan Martin has also motivated and impacted the writing of this book in many ways. He suggested the idea of a book in the first place and, as a college instructor, felt that I should pursue writing.

While reviewing the specific content of this book, many individuals put forth exceptional effort. Attorney Timothy Chevalier and his wife, Codie, offered many helpful ideas about the flow of the information and were willing, at many points, to confront me with needed criticism. Dr. David Smock dissected a large portion of the book and exposed several key weak points and at least one major error. Vernon Sorenson digested the matter of the book very thoroughly and offered many helpful reflections. Dr. Robert Perrotti also worked diligently on the refining stages of the book despite his strained health.

Although there is not space here to thank all those who participated in the development of this book, two individuals stand out. Physicist Chris Clarke and Professor Deborah Goldsborough both assessed the entire content of the book in great detail. Chris not only assessed the scientific conclusions and language of the book but also reworked most of my calculations to verify accuracy. Deborah Goldsborough went through the book with impressive precision, marking logical discontinuities and issues in language mechanics.

Above all, God—who is the proper Author of any true wisdom within this book—has blessed me with a patient and brilliant spouse who has labored diligently to make this insightful resource a reality. Liana also invested hundreds of hours, in this project. As always, her encouragement has been pivotal.

PREFACE

In recent decades, public education in the United States has become increasingly secularized. Many Americans have even been convinced that religious discussion at a public institution is unconstitutional. Not only is that common sentiment untrue, but the removal of religious discussion in any thinking society is impossible. As long as human minds are functioning well, there will always be religious discussion. In modern usage the term "secular" is used to denote an absence of religion, but the essential meaning of the word is "temporal" (as opposed to eternal). In other words, secular reasoning tends to be—by definition—shortsighted and pragmatic in its emphasis. And although secular humanism appears to be more pragmatic, it is in fact, a religion—the new stealthy state religion of the American public schools.

Since the inception of the term, secularism has claimed to be a way of thinking "independent" of Christian principles. The irony is that any alternate religion is defined that way. If we ignore traditional Christian values and focus on immediate circumstances to seek out a more convenient way of doing things, then we are just swapping out eternal doctrines for shallow, susceptible ones—it is religion all the same and a poor substitute.

Everyone falls into one of three categories. Some are religious outright, some claim a religion that does not honestly reflect their personal beliefs, and some deny being religious at all. As individuals of any culture, we have one thing in common: we are religious. For this reason it is impossible to keep religion out of the government, because it is impossible for a competent human being to be without core values. And it is inevitable that core values will be expressed.

Although the government has no rightful jurisdiction in matters of the church, religion will forever be a driving force of government. Separation of church and state can only be logically suggested or implemented one way because it is only genuinely possible one way. The chief aspiration of those who seeded the glory of America was a church free of government interference. No true patriot ever dreamt of a government free of religious influence, and it will frankly never exist. The First Amendment prohibits government from forming or promoting religious *establishments*, but religious *principles* must ever remain necessarily central to government. The pursuit of a fair and ordered government is in its very nature religious. Government is simply an outgrowth of religious principles. To deny the vital role of religion within the government is naïve at best—and in most cases plain dishonest.

My generation, Gen X, and those following have experienced a new and furtive form of indoctrination. Unlike the New England Primers and the McGuffey Readers used for many generations of the past, the textbooks of my generation claimed to be neutral regarding the spiritual aspects of life. How else would we *expect* evil to be introduced? Darkness has long been a fitting symbol of evil, because evil is deceptive in its nature. The most destructive evil is the kind that can pass itself off quietly not only as harmless, but good or virtuous—such as neutrality.

The document that initiated public education in the United States made it patently clear that the primary goal of American public education was for new generations to learn

Christian Scripture for the sake of avoiding deceptive evils. Yet, Christian texts have been gradually stripped from the classrooms, and ostensibly neutral "secular" materials have taken their place. The dreaded scenario that American public education was introduced to avoid is now a reality. And to make matters worse, the same institution that was conceived as a spiritual guardian has become a spiritual slaughterhouse, critically in need of some long overdue revisions.

The American culture, along with many world cultures, is experiencing this glaring philosophical and moral decay. Even as the world's technology advances, our margin of uncluttered time has ironically narrowed, and a fierce cycle of personal disconnect and spiritual deception has quietly gained momentum. It is a real and bad trade off that we can learn to decline and successfully exit.

INTRODUCTION

The universe is an accident. Really? It seems odd that life has no meaning, that natural science reeks of hopelessness, and that common sense fails us at every turn. As we make our way through the 21st century, a dank cloth of learned opinion tightens, threatening to douse the embers of vital faith. The faith of our fathers has been dismissed as a worn-out ideal, and in its absence we find ourselves wading chin-deep through a slop of trendy opinions masquerading as reality or worse, truth. At the end of the day, breathing sells as the grandest achievement of all. Is there no more to the story?

The recent surge of technology carries a flood of nifty and helpful products, but as terabytes of information zip through mechanical processors, *human* comprehension grows shallower by the day. In effect, we have ditched the search for deep implications at the onramp of the information superhighway. With data racing at us from a thousand directions, we find our thoughts in shreds—and long, hard thinking is no longer practical. Here's the pitiful bottom line: Whether or not there is more to the story or even a story at all, people have little space to care! But we must, for our lives are far too valuable. It is high time to get traction, to own hope, to know truth.

Science is a cherished gift and an impressive tool, but it fails at providing answers to our deepest questions. Granted, a few arrogant scientists will always buck at the thought of such limitations, but it is a fact. All the field study and scientific investigation in the world will not yield ultimate answers—

science by nature is open-ended. And thus we need to search beyond science. Here is our dilemma. We crave bedrock to build our lives upon, but science turns a deaf ear to our plea. Where do we *go* from here? Some suggest that we resign the search for purpose altogether, but for warm-blooded souls that is not a legitimate option.

So, if science cannot unearth a decent purpose for living, does it bar the way to one? An army of voices has been echoing throughout recorded ages a bold message of hope. What does science have to say about it? There is a Book that has stood stout as a lighthouse against centuries of pounding breakers. What of it? If the Book is true, then we have our answers. Some find that option too plain to accept; others find it too plain to deny. Could it be that simple? Here is the critical question each of us must answer: Is it plausible that this holy Book is genuinely all that it seems to be?

Many religions and philosophies present ideas about life as we experience it and what happens or does not happen after this life. Some deny the existence of spiritual things altogether. Whatever your particular position may be, if the basic message of the Bible is true, we all have a judgment day appointed in the future. And if the basic message of the Bible is true, our beliefs and preferences will certainly not alter the reality of that day. We are assured, "It is appointed unto men once to die, but after this the judgment" (Hebrews 9:27). Are you ready for that day? You certainly *can* be ready. Of all the possible applications of *Exit the Spiral*, that preparation for eternity is by far the most vital to the reader's true well-being.

Jesus Christ presented two pointed questions that are still very relevant today. He asked: "What shall it profit a man, if he shall gain the whole world, and lose his own soul? Or what shall a man give in exchange for his soul?" (Mark 8:36-37).

Jesus' first question presents a strong contrast between gaining the world and losing your soul. This contrast is very appropriate because the world is full of things that can distract us from the most important matters of life. All the wealth and conveniences in the world are only hollow illusions compared to eternity. Psalm 49 puts it this way: "They that trust in their wealth, and boast themselves in the multitude of their riches; None of them can by any means redeem his brother, nor give to God a ransom for him." One human soul is worth more than the combined wealth of the world.

Jesus' second question flows naturally from His first and is perhaps the most penetrating question in all of life: What can you give in exchange for your soul? The correct answer to this second question is the same as the answer to the first—"nothing." The Bible makes it patently clear at many points that each and every one of us has a guilty soul. If we will be truly honest before God, we each know—as the Bible says—that "All we like sheep have gone astray" (Isaiah 53:6) that "all have sinned, and come short of the glory of God" (Romans 3:23). A guilty soul needs more than repair—it needs replacement. We need an exchange for our soul.

That is why Jesus came; He gave His life for ours. He took the blame for our wrongs. He paid the price that we could not pay. He *did* what we could never do. Romans 5:6 celebrates, "For when we were yet without strength, in due time Christ died for the ungodly." Romans 5:8 continues: "while we were yet sinners, Christ died for us." First Peter 3:18 reveals that "Christ also hath once suffered for sins, the just for the unjust, that he might bring us to God."

God's laws are for our good. When we sin, we violate His laws and set up for pain and failure. The truth abbreviated from James 1:15 is that "sin, when it is finished ... death." God cares deeply about whether we sin because He loves us, because He has a much better vision for our lives, and because our sin hurts others that He loves. To resolve properly the consequences of our sin, we would be destined for an eternity in Hell. Revelation 20:15 specifies that "whosoever was not found written in the book of life was cast into the lake of fire" (a future event).

All the work necessary to fully redeem and secure our souls forever was done in the ministry of Jesus Christ. Hebrews 1:3 tells us that "he ... by himself purged our sins." It is Christ alone who can redeem a soul. We cannot save ourselves. Ephesians 2:8-9 summarizes: "by grace are ye saved through faith; and that not of yourselves: it is the gift of God: Not of works, lest any man should boast."

This amazing grace of God is offered freely to every individual regardless of race or record. But it must be requested. You are free to accept or decline. God does not twist arms, nor does He disregard our will. If you sincerely want to be forgiven of your sin in the person of Jesus Christ, then just ask. "Ask, and it shall be given you" (Matthew 7:7). Admit to God that you need a Savior and accept what the Lord Jesus has already done for you. If you accept your need of a Savior and call out for His grace, you are promised salvation. Romans 10:13 promises that "whosoever shall call upon the name of the Lord shall be saved." The Lord Jesus will forgive and secure all those who sincerely receive His finished work—His own pure blood offered for us.

Jesus died for our sins, but He also rose from the dead confirming that His work conquered sin, death, and Hell. His Spirit will literally live *with* us who accept His grace; and *He* will overcome sin in our lives as we yield to Him day to day.

We are *eternally secure* in Jesus Christ from the first moment that we receive Him as Savior, but it is our *free privilege* to grow *with* Him from that moment on. In Colossians 1:27 we find that the most valuable discovery we can enjoy in *this* world is simply "Christ in you." That is a find that will never lose any of its value. Hebrews 13:8 confirms that Jesus Christ is "the same" yesterday, and today, and forever. This statement of Christ's enduring nature has a profoundly *spiritual* import, and we are also about to see that the utility of *science* is inextricably dependent upon this fact.

CHAPTER 1
REASONABLE PROOF

—Defining the essence of reasonable proof is a necessary and foundational prerequisite for our study of needed revisions to secular thought. Parents and legal guardians willingly entrust educators with a sacred responsibility of passing *knowns* to upcoming generations, yet that trust has too often been violated by the dogma of certain unsubstantiated philosophies. We understand well the importance of discriminating between fact and fiction. When untried and unprovable concepts are assumed to be tried and proven, they are like dangerous hidden sink holes upon which we could regrettably build. All the same, adults—like children in a classroom—continue to absorb the same hollow philosophies through various media outlets. We are taught that secular explanations are *proven* explanations; but after critical examination of the supposed bases of these concepts, it appears evident that there is a serious need to reexamine what proof actually is.

LIMITS OF PROOF

As the moments of our lives pass, every particle of nature takes the witness stand.[a] Their testimony is bright and univocal, but a skeptical jury demands proof.[b] It is only

---

[a] Psalm 19:1–4
[b] Romans 1:19–22

natural then to ask, "Proof of what?" Here we come to an uncanny issue—there is no point on which to fix the crosshairs of investigation. All space, mass, and time broadcast an undivided testimony that affirms the meaning of nature—not the meaning of a single detail, but of the whole deal—the entire universe and everything in it!

All the classic instruments of forensics swivel wildly out of control. The question is too broad, the evidence too massive. The concept of proof implies that there is a *subset* of information that can be specified and restricted *within* other known information. There is no sense in searching for some unusual detail, when all we have to work with is stuff that bears a standardized signature. Proving a thing necessarily pigeonholes it. The atheist philosopher Friedrich Nietzsche admitted, "If one were to prove this God of Christians to us, we should be even less able to believe in him."[1] If the combined witness of all nature is not sufficient to make the case, why should anyone expect a *person* to convince such a jury?[a]

At what point should evidence be considered broad enough to end a conversation? Some would argue—through their actions—that there is no such point. What this means practically is that the degree of known-but-rejected evidence can be too *broad* to hope for any other kind of proof. Simply put, hardened *doubt* can make even the strongest cases impossible to prove.

The human soul has an exceptional ability to decide for or against certain things.[b] Sometimes there are very sound reasons behind human decisions, while at other times there

---

[a] Psalm 14:1
[b] Genesis 2:16; Revelation 22:17

seems to be little reason at all. Whether or not a reason surfaces clearly, we can remain certain that decisions are always driven by motives.ᵃ And, in turn, unrelenting *doubts* are the offspring of a particular motive—a dark one!ᵇ

Reliable ancient Scripture describes the infant days of our world as a pristine environmentᶜ that quickly became corrupted by unreasonable doubt.ᵈ That doubt slithered from motives that would ultimately poison the whole of nature.ᵉ Authority totes responsibility, and in this case the luggage was immense! Although the decision to doubt was a personal one, the offender, Adam, had been given personal responsibility for managing the natural world.ᶠ When he acted in selfish pride, nature felt the consequences.ᵍ Throughout recorded history, we have witnessed the resulting decay—both moral and physical. Nature, on its grandest scale, provides us with an intensely sobering picture. Physicist Brian Greene provides this definition of the universe: "Incredible order at the beginning is what started it all off, and we have been living through the gradual unfolding toward higher disorder ever since."² The snowballing degree of *doubt* in our present society is nothing more than the spiritual parallel of this decay.ʰ

While having way too much known-but-rejected evidence certainly poses an important limitation in our search to prove things true, our search for proof can also meet a

---

ᵃ Matthew 7:16; 12:34–35
ᵇ Proverbs 28:1; Titus 1:15; Revelation 21:8
ᶜ Genesis 1:31
ᵈ Genesis 3:1–19
ᵉ 1 John 2:16
ᶠ Genesis 1:26
ᵍ Genesis 3:16–19; Romans 8:18–23
ʰ 2 Timothy 3:13

much more conventional barrier—too *little* information. We shelve certain ideas on the basis of insufficient information. This seems reasonable, but it's hard to practice. No one likes admitting ignorance about a given subject. So, naturally, we are tempted to make stuff up. This is too often the case in our scientific community.

After writing emphatically about the *science* of origins, biologist Richard Dawkins reveals: "We can hope for nothing more than speculation when the events we are talking about took place 4 billion years ago and took place, moreover, in a world that must have been radically different from that which we know today."[3] Although 4 billion years ago sounds suspiciously like "once upon a time," it follows logically from the statement that scientists who use such a time frame cannot speak of origins with any data-based confidence (which is the hallmark of true science) and therefore must assume there is only piddling information available.

EXPECTATIONS FOR PROOF

Although clearly we cannot prove a thing beyond all possible doubt, we tend to expect a certain minimum amount of evidence before taking a claim seriously. Oddly, this has *not* been the recent practice of average biologists, astrophysicists, and psychologists. As bizarre as this statement may seem, an unbiased look at the available data leads to no other conclusion. The expectation that these scientists would demand reasonable evidence to support their assertions has been crushed time after time. Often in place of fact, we find naked devotion.

If a theory's predictions fail and fail and fail again, what else do we have to work with? Biologist Massimo Pigliucci concludes: "Prediction is the only test we have that enables us to discriminate between adequate and inadequate models of the world."[4] In this way, humanistic models of the natural and social sciences must submit to the same test as scriptural prophecy—are the predictions confirmed or disconfirmed? Here we find a stark contrast.

Reliable ancient Scripture predicted that the nation of Israel would, at an appointed time, take her rightful place as a focal point of world powers.[a] Then for almost 1,900 years, the Jewish people were scattered throughout the nations—dramatically out of focus. Here was an outstanding challenge for the predictive power of Scripture. Could the prophecy still be fulfilled? Then, on May 14, 1948, it happened![b] Israel became a nation again. After almost 19 centuries that blurred the lines of possibility, our planet witnessed clarion

---

[a] Isaiah 11:12; Jeremiah 31:10; Ezekiel 11:17; 34:12–13, 21; Micah 2:12; Psalm 147:2; Acts 1:6–7
[b] Isaiah 66:8

fulfillment. This kind of prophetic accuracy is the rule throughout the Scripture.[a] Theologian Hal Lindsey points out that Old Testament prophets were required to produce true prophesies under penalty of death. He says, "They passed the test—summa cum laude."[5]

The humanistic philosophies plaguing the natural and social sciences today have no such record. Of all the poisoned ideas corrupting these sciences, the opinions of Charles Darwin are among the most destructive. If Darwin's theory of natural progression were sound, we would have expected certain things. *He* himself expected certain things and was sorely disappointed to find that they did not appear.

Where are the fossils? Charles Darwin wondered, "Why then is not every geological formation and every stratum full of such intermediate links? Geology *assuredly* does not reveal any such finely graduated organic chain; and this, perhaps, is the most obvious and gravest objection which can be urged against my theory"[6] (emphasis added). Darwin realized that the whole *chain* of fossils that he predicted was "assuredly" missing.[7] He felt that this issue would prove to be the "gravest" embarrassment his conception of evolution would ever have to justify. And, as a rule, modern scientists agree that the fossil record remains the most direct evidence of life history available. Dawkins[p10] confirms that "fossils provide us with our only direct evidence of the animals and plants of the distant past."[8]

To Darwin's dismay the fossil record introduces all the major species groups in one grand entrance generally called the Cambrian explosion. The Cambrian stratum seems to

---

[a] Deuteronomy 18:22

imply that the diversity of living things sprang suddenly into existence. While this evidence conforms well with the written history found in reliable ancient Scripture,[a] it provides a real crisis for Darwin's concept of evolution. The central concept of evolution requires very gradual changes. Biologist Ernst Mayr marvels, "Yet the facts are astonishingly different from this assumption!" He explains: "The variety of realized body plans was greater in the Cambrian than it is now. Furthermore, no fundamentally new body plan has originated in the 500 million years since the Cambrian."[9] Earnst Mayr was a key representative in developing the modern synthesis of evolutionary theory—the *source* of fundamental doctrine for the Darwinist community.

To grasp the concept of how far evolution is from explaining Cambrian data, consider Mayr's desperate attempt to do so—all body plans were soft bodied before the Cambrian explosion. There's no bones about it, he proposes that all species that appear in the Cambrian stratum developed skeletons around or *inside* existing soft-bodied animals. He also proposes the question many of us would have, "One would have to ask, what caused this sudden skeletonization of so many unrelated phyla?"[10] Apparently an entire army of completely distinct soft-bodied animals developed skeletons at nearly the same time.

Although there is no scientific reason for the synchronized development of these quite dissimilar skeletons, Darwinists have an obligation to explain why the huge variety of fossilized skeletons is infused into the Cambrian stratum. Mayr does not entertain questions such as why did these animals wait to grow skeletons side by side? And why do soft-

---

[a] Genesis 1:1–28, 7:21–23; Exodus 20:11

bodied animals no longer spontaneously develop skeletons? Rather, Mayr is content to speculate why the animals would have *needed* the skeletons.

Although Darwin hoped the fossil record would be the most disheartening illustration of his concept's predictive incompetence, it turned out to be merely the first in a smorgasbord of habitual disappointments—development of variation, genetic heritage, radiocarbon dating, minimum complexity, and the practical *utility* of natural selection to name a few.[a]

Consider the concept of natural variation development. Darwinism predicts that natural mutations will consistently create variation to provide options for natural selection to work with. Unless new, beneficial variations develop, evolution helplessly runs laps!

East Africa's Lake Victoria holds a unique and diverse collection of fish known as cichlids. *Five hundred* unique and wonderfully distinct varieties of a certain cichlid group occur in this geologically young lake, so they almost certainly had a common ancestor.[11] The diversity of these isolated fish indicates an impressive capacity for variation. Where did it come from? The restricted time frame makes the possibility of brand-new mutations more challenging than ever. Science writer Carl Zimmer suggests, "The cichlids that colonized Lake Victoria entered a much more stable place.... They could rapidly evolve specialized ways of living and not get punished for their change."[12] In order for this to work, the cichlids would have had to store up useful genetic potential *before*

---

[a] Proverbs 19:21

entering the lake. Darwinists expect this kind of variation to develop naturally through mutations. Should *we?*

December 22, 1938: The phone rang at the museum where Marjorie Courtenay-Latimer was curator ... a familiar voice; it was her friend Hendrick Goosen, a local trawler captain. He had something for Marjorie to take a look at. Although she was busy at the time working on some fossilized reptiles, she decided that with Christmas weekend on the way, she would go ahead and break away for a little while to wish the captain and crew a merry Christmas. She was in for quite a surprise. When she stepped on board the trawler, a slimy, blue *something* caught her attention. There lying on the deck was a living fossil—a fish that was supposed to have gone extinct at the time of the dinosaurs. She would soon learn that the 127-pound fish that intrigued her was none other than coelacanth (seel-uh-canth)—a taxon that supposedly linked fish with tetrapods. The years must have been good to old coelacanth, for he looked surprisingly young (Darwinistically speaking).

But here's the problem. According to secular evolutionists coelacanth had been swimming in an almost identical form for 2,000 to 4,000 times the age of East Africa's Lake Victoria. That means that these fish would have had 2,000 to 4,000 times as long to express diversity as compared to the Lake Victoria cichlids! If the diversity that's necessary for Darwinian progress developed naturally, the *same* young look would take a whole lot of diligent natural primping. The pressures of the environment would have to be precise enough to thread a genetic needle.

To bring us up to date, there are two very similar live species of coelacanth that can be distinguished under the microscope or by color. One or the other has been discovered in the following countries: Comoros, Kenya, Mozambique,

Tanzania, Madagascar, and Indonesia.[13] We have found no tight niche to genetically freeze coelacanth through the supposed eons. Where's the diversity?

Although "living fossils" like coelacanth are not uncommon,[14] one reigns supreme—Darwinists' granddaddy of all prehistoric fossils, the blue-green algae. Many of Darwin's modern-day disciples claim that this microbe has been in existence up to *seven times* as long as any other life form! These little critters *still* look the same. Zimmer[p14] reveals: "The oldest actual fossils ... look exactly like living blue-green algae."[15] Mayr[p13] agrees: "What is most remarkable about the cyanobacteria [blue-green algae] is their morphological stasis."[16] Morphological stasis in this context means that the bodies of blue-green algae are not changing much over time.

The tightly limited degree of variation stands out as pure phenomenon. Blue-green algae experience an impressively quick lifecycle; and when influential evolutionists multiply it by enough time to reenact the events of East Africa's Lake Victoria 35,000 times, the concept of Darwinism begs for *change*. Since blue-green algae continue to have such phenomenal success in neighborhood ponds and household aquariums, we can be confident that they certainly have the *room* to change if variation was available. All this to say ... biologically necessary variations are not *observed* to arise naturally! This logically suggests that evolution will naturally function within *defined* limits caused by *existing* variation.

Let's bring this concept home. Scientists struggle with the idea of genetic consistency because things in our world break down naturally. Dawkins[p10] insists, "More biologists agree that stasis is a real phenomenon than agree about its causes."[17] Reliable ancient Scripture tells us that biological diversity was produced by authoritative *words*.ᵃ We are reminded throughout that these words flow from the ultimate Rock of stability and that they carry with them characteristics of an *eternal* personality.ᵇ

When we apply what has long been written about the personality of the Author of life, we find that we have an authorized Record of the preserving power necessary to keep a relevant portion of genetic material intact. And so, the observed tendency toward genetic stasis confirms the natural expectation of reliable ancient Scripture. After years of prophetic accuracy to deepen its beauty, these modern jewels of confirmation adorn the Scripture still more brilliantly.ᶜ

In contrast, the *blight* this data inflicts on Darwin's concept of progression is much less flattering. The whole point of Darwinistic evolution was to show how biological complexity could be the result of natural *progress*. Darwin had no interest in a stale (or static) theory; his goal was to explain a means of natural *progress*. We now realize that such expectations are entirely incredible.

As it turns out, the modern scientific definition of evolution no longer carries Darwin's central idea. Dawkins confesses, "Contrary to earlier prejudices, there is nothing inherently progressive about evolution."[18] Although he suggests that certain natural relationships could ideally result in progressive *appearances*, the point remains that learned scientists know that evolution possesses no definite mechanisms for significant progress. Book-smart Darwinists

---

ᵃ Genesis 1:11, 20, 24, 26; Psalm 29:1–9; Hebrews 11:3
ᵇ Deuteronomy 32:4, 33:27; Numbers 23:19; Psalm 119:160; 1 Timothy 1:17; Hebrews 13:8
ᶜ Isaiah 55:12

are forced to believe that biological structure in general is a spontaneous side-effect and ultimately a natural fluke. Biologist Douglas J. Futuyma accepts that "Today 'evolution' has come to mean, simply, 'change.'"[19] In other words, we have found that the idea of natural *progress* cannot be reconciled with accessible data. As a result of those findings, the term "evolution" has been grossly mangled to a point of definitive uselessness.[a]

That said, modern evolution seems to present little challenge to Scripture. Yet, the concept of natural progression lingers like a foul rag that blindfolds an ungodly fraction of the scientific community. Worst of all, at the end of the day, Darwin's cherished concept has never even *attempted* to answer the core question of biology—the *origin* of life—and thus the title of his classic work, *Origin of a Species*, has a legitimately misleading flavor. Evolution has always been about changes in *existing* life forms. Though the expectation reigns supreme, there has *never* been a real provision for explaining the origin of life by means of evolution. It is a conflict of terms. Pigliucci[p11] clarifies, "Evolution is not a theory of the origin of life."[20]

As abysmal as this empty story is, Darwinism is not alone in having a hollow bottom. Many other oversold "scientific" fields do as well.[b]

For example, a current doctrine of psychology teaches that all morality sprouts from a desire for well-being. In other words, consequences themselves draw the line between right and wrong. (Although we sometimes act as if this were true, we ought to *know* better.) This doctrine is referred to as

---

[a] Genesis 49:4; Romans 1:22
[b] Isaiah 54:17; 1 Timothy 6:20

consequentialism. The ultimate goal of consequentialism is to prove that moral truth *exists* as a product of natural laws and independent of a holy Creator. What is most noteworthy about this teaching is that it offers no answers—like Darwinism it sports a hollow bottom. In his book *The Moral Landscape*, psychologist and neuroscientist Sam Harris expects that "consequentialism is less a method of answering moral questions than it is a claim about the status of moral truth."[21] That means that the concept claims to describe morals without offering anything that *works*. It's like a physics theory that can't produce any reliable data. Shouldn't we scrap such nonsense? There must be real answers that we can really use.[a] After all, life here is *short*.

To find the most massive of all "scientific" disappointments, however, we must pay a brief visit to the field of astrophysics. Astrophysics is the field of science that deals with physical events in cosmic space. Of all the questions we have launched at this field, the greatest concerns the beginning of time and space. Scientists often tell us that it all started with the "big bang"—words that sound awkwardly like something from an elementary school text. Greene[p9] explains what he believes is the foundation of the physical sciences, however: "We have now come to the place where the buck finally stops. *The ultimate source of order, of low entropy, must be the big bang itself.*"[22]

Are we missing something here? Once again our search leads us to a hollow bottom; there really is not even a *claim* for the beginning. Greene understands that a "common misconception is that the big bang provides a theory of cosmic origins." He admits, "It doesn't."[23] In terms of the known

---
[a] Deuteronomy 30:11–14; Psalm 94:18; 119:105

physical behaviors of nature, the big bang concept can only represent part of a *chain* reaction—leaving the real cause of beginning in some other unknown *universe*.[a] How's that for a hollow bottom?

The essence of reasonable proof expects—or even demands—certain evidences. Without such evidences, data-based confidence is not a logical possibility. The secular mainstream of the scientific community has demonstrated its naked devotion to groundless ideas. If professional naturalists choose to believe these dark ideas, they are still scientists no less. But they should not confuse these shady concepts with legitimate science—for they certainly are *not*.

---

[a] Hebrews 11:3

CONCLUSIONS WITH PROOF

A trove of information relating to a common theme can amount to evidence. When ample evidence gravitates toward a common point and laces together smoothly, it forms a discrete bundle that we call a conclusion. When we reason about a subject, we are actually setting out to capture and hold the value of a *conclusion*. Unless our study yields conclusions of some kind, it is a waste. We *ache* for answers to live by, but each of us has only a limited opportunity to search out such answers. Ideally every conclusion would be based on concrete proof; in the real world, however, building a flawless mound of scientific evidence becomes, at points, hopeless.

The work of research must be carried out diligently and to the greatest extent possible. Yet, as a matter of practicality, we must produce many dynamic conclusions—conclusions that spring forcibly from our concentrated *sense* of truth. Although we all must base our lives on a footing of such dynamic conclusions, science prefers highly mechanical methods of proof.

Though scientific proof cannot penetrate a shell of hardened doubt, it does provide well-defined terms for its evidence. This allows for effective communication of proof, to whatever degree it will be accepted. A certain Hungarian proverb says, "The believer is happy; the doubter is wise." It is reasonable to think that a believer who finds truth is happy; yet it is hard to see how a doubter can be wise, because the truly devoted skeptic, by definition, must always know *nothing*. So the proverb is wrong: It is both satisfying *and* wise to adopt conclusions (i.e., believe).

Reliable ancient Scripture exposes the causes and events of biological and cosmic origins.[a] Given the limits of our current technology, it would be otherwise impossible for us to know the particular details that are revealed in the written Record. All that we *do* know, however, leads to a common reinforcing conclusion—nature was created![b]

Nature sprang into existence as a passive subject responding to an active Cause. Establishing the actual *identity* of the Cause requires a dynamic conclusion. The conclusion, however, that *a* vibrant supernatural cause exists is purely mechanical. Scientific investigation has reached conclusions about the natural world that plainly testify to the existence of a vibrant supernatural first cause. *Life cannot simply generate from non-living material nor can mass be naturally created.* These are well-established central principles of science. Although science does not actually allow for truly *final* conclusions, these principles represent the firmest conclusions real science has to offer.

Biology is based on cell theory. By all legitimate scientific standards we now *know* that matter *cannot* spontaneously come to life! Biological creation myths such as spontaneous generation/abiogenesis are not science. Science is based on *observation.* Observation shows us clearly that life is a gift. Mayr[p13] confirms this: "We now realize that, owing to the current composition of the Earth's atmosphere, such spontaneous generation of new life … can no longer take place."[24]

We *know* that life does not spring into existence in the real world. Mayr claims that in a world without oxygen there

---

[a] Genesis 1:1–28; Exodus 20:11; Exodus 31:17; Psalm 89:11
[b] Psalm 19:1

may be some mystical chance of this event.[25] But, cell theory forbids it. Cell theory is the powerhouse of all biological study, and the field has no greater conclusion.

In physics the first law of thermodynamics carries similar clout. The first law of thermodynamics states that the energy of our universe, although it can take the form of matter, can never be destroyed or created. Physicists often refer to this law simply as the conservation of energy. It is the hook upon which the whole study of mass currently hangs. And its future looks bright.[a]

As physicists attempt to develop new theories, a key step in the process is calculating a broad spectrum of scenarios in order to identify the possible contradictions for their theories. In this process, the first law of thermodynamics stands out as an unusually good benchmark. In other words, physicists use the first law of thermodynamics as a trusty standard.[26] It determines whether or not new concepts are reasonable. Because of its proven value, we can confidently expect the first law to hold in years to come. Like cell theory in biology, this essential *conclusion* of physics logically implies a supernatural beginning.

Nature does not produce energy, and yet energy exists. By all current scientific standards, we *know* that nature was created by a vibrant supernatural cause. Accordingly, the *most* eminent scientists,[27] both historic and modern, have almost unanimously recognized a supernatural Person as the necessary first cause.

Moving beyond these general principles, we find an assortment of highly particular scientific conclusions that are also consistent with reliable ancient Scripture. Darwin

---

[a] Proverbs 3:19; Isaiah 45:18; Colossians 1:17

believed cells were unrealistically simple. He pictured cells as basic building blocks with a few elementary processes occurring inside. Our current understanding of cell components and processes devastates his primitive idea.

"Simple" life forms are not a legitimate topic for any serious scientific discussion. Small does not mean crude. Some of the most remarkable complexity of life is neatly packaged *inside* cells. Digital information comparable to the content of *Encyclopedia Britannica* has been programmed into even the most "basic" cell.[28] Here we find an impressive array of microscopic machinery. At this level we can peek at the actual molecules and atoms. Indeed, *all* the fantastic structures inside the fundamental unit of life represent a particular arrangement of atoms.

As we begin to understand the chemical reactions that take place inside cells, we are approaching conclusions. Biologist Michael J. Behe affirms, "When we descend from the level of a whole animal (such as a beetle) or whole organ (such as an eye) to the molecular level, then in many cases we *can* make a judgment on evolution because all of the parts of many discreet molecular systems *are* known."[29] Behe presents the powerful case in a book-length discussion appropriately titled *Darwin's Black Box.*

The glut of biochemical information flooding scientific journals has sparked renewed interest in intelligent design. In his book *The Design Revolution*, biochemist William A. Dembski informs us:

> It's not just that certain biological systems are so complex that we can't imagine how they evolved by Darwinian pathways. Rather, we can show conclusively that they could not have evolved by

direct Darwinian pathways and that indirect Darwinian pathways, which have always been on much less stable ground, are utterly without empirical support.³⁰

By examining the inner workings of a cell, we can confidently reveal an endless network of holes in Darwin's concept of progression. At the same time we deepen our respect for the Designer's wisdom.ᵃ

Genes provide us with another highly particular case to reinforce the statements of reliable ancient Scripture. Darwin thought that all living things were literally related. He thought that everything that has ever lived could be traced back to one literal, physical ancestor. This bizarre concept flew in the face of established science.

A century before Darwin, biologist Carolus Linnaeus had developed a system for classifying plants and animals. It was not Linnaeus' intention to tie all life forms into some literal, physical relationship. Linnaeus arranged species into larger categories based on physical similarities. The goal of this project was to flush out reoccurring themes—the patterns preferred by nature's Designer. To Linnaeus, the themes of nature were a useful insight into the wisdom of her Author.ᵇ

Darwin interpreted these same large categories as branches of literal, physical descent—his tree of life. Modern evolutionists have continued to assume that, if Darwinian evolution were true, such branches (clades) could each be traced back to a unique, literal ancestor. Hybrids between major species groups would be logically impossible. Dawkins[p10]

ᵃ Psalm 8:3–9; 139:17–18; Luke 12:27–28
ᵇ Romans 1:20; 1 Corinthians 14:10

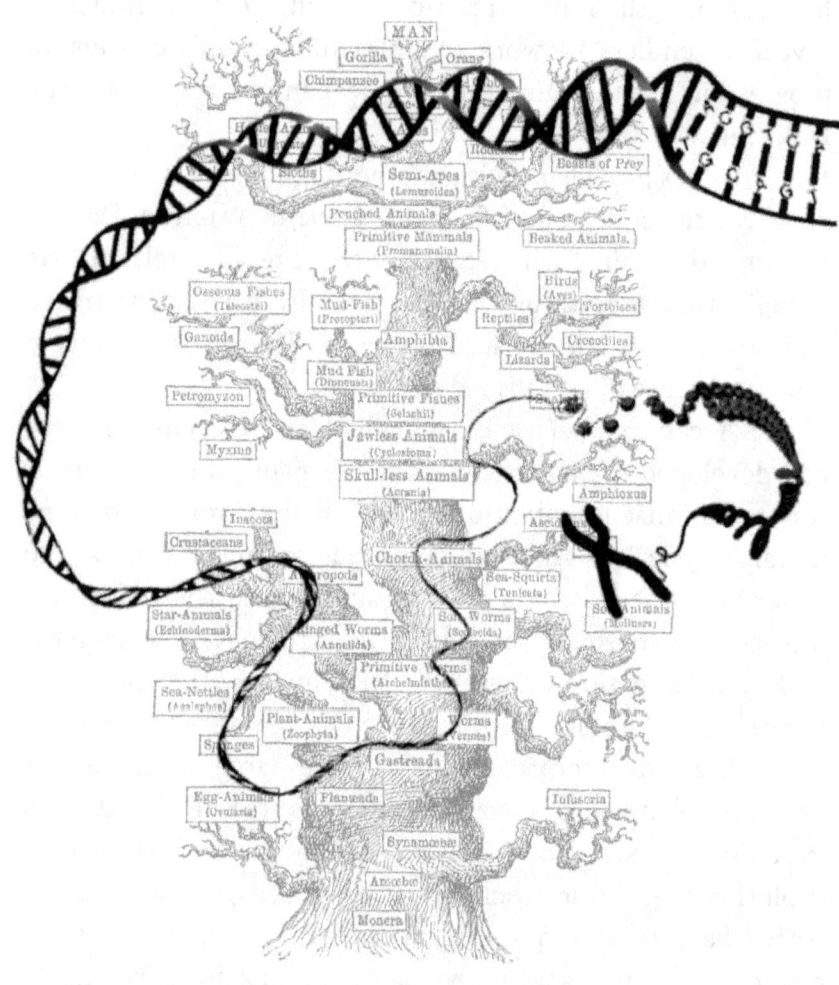

insists, "Biological evolution above the species level is always divergent."[31] There really is no other logical option for Darwinism to work with. As we discussed earlier, however, there is no fossil evidence to support a gradual development of the species groups in the first place. There is no literal thread to link groups in a Darwinistic fashion. And so, in order to defend Darwin's tree-of-life concept, many evolutionists have turned their attention to genetics.

Here, once again, Darwinism has been dealt a hammering blow. The conclusions of genetic research have, by all rights, put the last nail in Darwinism's coffin. Groups of species that *appear* to be similar are not nearly as similar as we thought! *Darwinists* are losing faith in their belief system. Biologists Gareth Nelson and Ron Platnick confess, "Darwinism ... is, in short, a theory that has been put to the test and found false."[32] This devastating conclusion comes from scientists who have worked to prove Darwinism *true* and have come up wanting.

Genetic evidence does not at all conform to Darwin's preconceptions about physical appearances. Modern genetic research has helped to conclusively refute the evolutionary relationships assumed by Darwinists. The verdict is clear. Accessible data gathered from genes and other molecules shows that Darwin's tree of life is nowhere to be found. This buries Darwin's concept of evolution. This, once again, should strengthen our respect for the Designer—especially His creativity.[a]

The firmest conclusions science has to offer should ideally represent *true* statements. Although science does not directly offer truth, conclusions represent statements that we

---

[a] Psalm 139:17–18

feel are true. Because the truth about real-world events must ultimately be felt, philosophers often argue that truth is only an illusion. Nature disagrees.[a]

The physical properties of light provide an unusually good illustration of ultimate truth. It is certainly not a coincidence that the Engineer of our universe selected light as the first created property. He even identifies with it personally![b] But what is it about light that makes it so phenomenal? As physicists continue to study the properties of light, the peculiar discoveries about it seem endless. Albert Einstein found that our concept of time *and* space are relative to the fixed speed of light. As we move through space our concept of time *changes* in proportion to our speed. This creates exotic results. All things are relative to one exception—light.

In fact, Einstein was more impressed by the *stability* of light than its effects on the universe. Although the name "relativity" stuck, Einstein originally intended to call his theory "invariance theory" to emphasize the impressively rigid properties of light.[33] Einstein knew that our personal perspective hinges on our relationship to light, and that the speed of light anchors reality.

Like truth, natural light is timeless.[c] If an individual were to approach the speed of light, time for that individual would be stretched. By traveling through space at near light speed, it would be possible to live decades during one typical earth day. Light itself is beyond time. Greene[p9] illustrates: "A

---

[a] Genesis 1:3; John 1:5
[b] 1 John 1:5
[c] Hebrews 13:8

watch worn by a particle of light would not tick at all."[34] And so eternity dangles closer than we realize.

Mathematically speaking, the smooth passage of time that we sense is almost quirky. On earth time seems to pass evenly only because we are all moving at roughly the same velocity. If our rate of motion significantly changed relative to one another, however, our watches would all fall out of sync. Even stranger, across astronomical distances of space, our motion relative to one another changes our version of the present entirely. For each of us, the day of our birth is still in the *present* somewhere in the universe. Greene continues: "Events, regardless of when they happen from any particular perspective, just *are*. They all exist. They eternally occupy their particular point in spacetime."[35] That is totally awesome! The past is etched into the very fabric of our universe, and in some very real way, our future is physically certain.

Scientific conclusions often lead us to truth's doorstep but never over the threshold. Truth may not flow naturally from science, but it is out there no less. Truly data-based conclusions get us in the neighborhood of truth, and we need to take them seriously. At the same time, though, we need to understand the proper limits of proof in order to establish fair expectations with which to develop our conclusions.

CHAPTER 1 REVIEW

STUDY NOTE: This chapter lays an important philosophical basis. Contrary to prevailing prejudices on all sides of the final truth debates, *absolute* proof is *not* a realistic possibility. Those searching for the truth must ultimately settle for whatever they consider *sufficient* evidence. The reader should take care to digest this foundational section carefully. It is a difficult but liberating chapter.
(See pages 195-197 for suggested answers).

THE LIMITS OF PROOF:
1. The figurative courtroom in the first paragraph refers to what?
2. Why are the "moments of our lives" significant in this courtroom?
3. How is the testimony of nature "bright"?
4. How is the testimony of nature "univocal"?
5. Give an example of proving something using a subset of information.
6. Imagine trying to prove by observation that each atom of the earth contains a nucleus. Why would such pursuit be an exercise in frustration?
7. Why would you tend to be suspicious of the philosophy of a person who felt it a personal responsibility to prove the existence of God?
8. When is evidence sufficient to end an investigative discussion?
9. Why would someone ignore clear evidence?
10. What is a key motive that drives unrelenting doubts?
11. If the first human couple drank a radioactive substance that caused hereditary mutations and the total loss of all their combined eye-forming genes, how would that effect the current human population?
12. Who were the first two humans according to the Bible?
13. What may be a powerful largescale illustration of the spiritual fall of humanity, and its ongoing consequences?
14. What is a <u>moral</u> equivalent to the universal decline toward disorder?
15. What is the most conventional barrier that prevents proof?
16. Why must secular evolutionists speculate rather than use factual evidence when discussing early life history?

CHAPTER 1 REVIEW 31

THE EXPECTATIONS FOR PROOF:
1. We will never prove anything beyond all doubt, but what should we require before taking claims seriously?
2. In what way do the natural and social sciences have to submit to the same test as Scripture?
3. If a person remains devoted to a theory after its predictions have habitually failed, is it reasonable to believe that such devotion is based in either logic or science?
4. On what date did Israel become a nation again?
5. In Old Testament times what was the penalty for prophets whose prophecies were shown to be untrue?
6. What did Charles Darwin hope geology would reveal?
7. Was Darwin convinced that there was a missing fossil link or chain?
8. What is the Cambrian Explosion?
9. What does the Cambrian explosion imply?
10. Who is Ernst Mayr?
11. What does Mayr suggest as an explanation for the sudden appearance of Cambrian fossils?
12. The fossil record shows that Darwin's predictions were invalid. What are 5 other areas of study that show this?
13. What is predicted by the concept of natural variation development?
14. How many varieties of cichlid evolved in East Africa's Lake Victoria?
15. What weird 127-pound blue fish was discovered in 1938?
16. According to secular evolutionists how long had coelacanth been swimming in an almost identical form (relative to Lake Victoria's history)?
17. What do secular evolutionists claim is the oldest living life form?
18. What did Ernst Mayr say is most remarkable about what he considers the earliest life form on earth?
19. If biologically necessary variations do *not* arise naturally, how does that affect the process of evolution?
20. How does genetic stasis confirm the implications of Scripture?
21. What was Darwin's central concept of evolution that is no longer supported by the modern scientific definition of evolution?
22. In what way does Darwinism have a "hollow bottom"?
23. What does consequentialism propose?
24. Where would we hope to find the cause of "the big bang"?

THE CONCLUSIONS WITH PROOF:
1. When we reason about a subject, what is the goal?
2. What are the "dynamic conclusions" referring to in this section?
3. What is an example of a "dynamic conclusion"?
4. Why is the saying "The believer is happy; the doubter is wise" wrong?
5. What does cell theory forbid?
6. What law states "energy cannot be created or destroyed"?
7. What do current scientific laws imply about origins of mass and life?
8. What have the greatest scientists concluded about the first cause?
9. What are the names of some great scientists who recognized overwhelming evidence of an intelligent Creator?
10. What life unit contains as much information as a large encyclopedia?
11. Can modern study of cell structure invalidate Darwin's theories?
12. Who developed a very useful system for classifying life forms?
13. What has genetic research found about Darwin's tree of descent?
14. Why do philosophers often argue that truth is only an illusion?
15. What provides an unusually good illustration of absolute truth?
16. What was Albert Einstein's original name for the theory of relativity?
17. What happens to a person who travels very quickly?
18. Why does our time pass evenly on earth (in other words we both lived for 365 days in 2018 and would not expect to live 700 days in that calendar year)?
19. Is your date of birth still in the present somewhere in the universe?

CHAPTER 2
MORAL TAPROOTS

—The truth of right and wrong matters profoundly. Secular concepts of an amoral universe breed and disseminate a vile alternative "morality" that poisons the human soul and decimates whole cultures. Whenever final authority is rejected, standards are negotiable—inane. The moral relativity propagated so aggressively in recent years serves best, in fact, as a mock means for justifying *failures* of personal integrity. True moral standards are *not* negotiable. Any reliable natural science must be built upon rigid, uncompromising physical laws; in much the same way the existence of any truly thriving society requires rigid, uncompromising moral principles. In the absence of such principles, cultural chaos is inevitable. Amorality—now professionally sanctioned—lies at the root of a wide assortment of popular but deceptive "scientific" misinformation.

IRRESPONSIBILITY

As modern schools wade deeper into trendy psychobabble, we are witnessing an immensely disturbing moral retardation of the coming generations. Academic achievement without personal integrity presents grave danger to society, and is at best a waste. While most educators are acutely aware of this fact, many modern public education systems have shied away from their moral duties. The looming dangers are innumerable. In the name of political correctness, moral *potency* has been sapped from public classrooms. The result: The future of *nations* is being jeopardized for the sake of a supercharged brand of tolerance.

When all hope that a person will behave properly seems *gone*, our only polite option is tolerance. Philosopher and theologian Norman Geisler agrees: "Tolerance is too weak—tolerance says, hold your nose and put up with them. Love says, reach out and help them."[1] When tolerance is sold as the highest moral code of a society, we can mark it down that that society has fallen into a desperate moral condition.

Tolerating wrong has consumed so much of our generation's attention that we have lost touch with what is *right*. While we were busy being tolerant, the morality of the rising generation has been systematically blurred, mucked, and molested. Our condition has become so desperate that some *secular* psychologists have even begun fighting for some kind of sane moral standard. For instance, atheist neuropsychologist Sam Harris[p19] asserts, "My claim is that there are right and wrong answers to moral questions, just as there are right and wrong answers to questions of physics, and such answers may one day fall within reach of the maturing sciences of mind."[2] If those sciences were ever perfected, the product would be a copy of the principles outlined in reliable ancient Scripture.[a] We do not need new technology to answer moral questions.[b] We need to appreciate what we already have. We need a mature sense of *responsibility*.

---

[a] Psalm 119:160
[b] Ecclesiastes 1:9

Irresponsibility breeds confusion.[a] To illustrate, let's look at the history of public education in the United States. The original *mission statement* of American public education has been discarded like an obsolete relic. On November 11, 1647, a document that would signify the birth of public education in this country was signed. The order is known as the "Old Deluder Satan Act." Here we find the original objective of this public education system:

> It being one chief project of that old deluder, Satan, to keep men from the knowledge of the *Scriptures,* as in former times by keeping them in an unknown tongue, so in these latter times by persuading from the use of tongues... *It is therefore ordered* that every township in this jurisdiction, after the Lord hath increased them to fifty households shall forthwith appoint one within their town to teach all such children as shall resort to him to write and read.[3] (Emphasis added.)

The number one objective of the American public education system was spiritual literacy—through the study of reliable ancient Scripture.

Even as America burns through billions of dollars in public education funding, the greatest fear of our ancestors has come upon us.[b] The result is that the average American youth hears more about reliable ancient Scripture at rock concerts than he does in the modern public classroom. The confusion this has caused is so severe that roles are being reversed[c]—

---

[a] Proverbs 15:19
[b] Deuteronomy 8:11; Psalm 9:17; 11:3
[c] Isaiah 5:20; 1 Peter 3:16

those who defend the original mission statement of American public education are accused of *subverting* the purposes of education.⁴ America has carelessly left behind her moral compass and wandered a long way in the wrong direction ever since. In our generation, American youth need public educators who will take on the responsibility of protecting the Truth against its misled/misleading enemies.

Irresponsibility hurts.[a] Anyone who has ever swung a hammer carelessly can testify that irresponsibility has a habit of coming back around to get us. Irresponsibility keeps much of the nation of Israel from her Physician. It's not that the Jewish people have been deprived of a Savior, but rather many have *chosen* to reject the prophesied Messiah.[b]

To this day, many orthodox Jews reject the Hope of the ages. Lindsey[p12] reasons, "Any person who hasn't come to see that his most basic problem is an inner spiritual one prefers a political deliverer to a spiritual one. It is not difficult, therefore, to understand the basic attitude [of many Jews] which rationalized away the prophetic portrait of the suffering Messiah." He stresses the point. "In their blindness they discounted more than *300 specific predictions* in their own sacred writings about this Messiah."⁵ (See *Appendix*.)

This is perhaps *the* most peculiar event in recorded history. After *centuries* of anticipation, all the messianic prophecies that the Jews had held above life itself suddenly came to pass.[c] The world is shaken by the immense prophetic fulfillment. [d] And somehow most the Jews themselves

---

[a] Proverbs 24:30–34; Matthew 25:30; Luke 25:45–47
[b] Matthew 23:37; Luke 13:34; Romans 10:19–21
[c] Luke 21:22; Acts 13:29
[d] Acts 17:6

shrugged it off. Irresponsibility has spiritually crippled many orthodox Jews. By persistently denying their spiritual needs, many Jews have literally lost their souls. How hard is it to admit our need of Christ? The cost of sin is real. The blood of Jesus Christ was shed for Jews, as it was for all mankind. What a *waste* is irresponsibility!

Irresponsibility drove Darwin to invent his concept of secular evolution. Contrary to popular belief science did *not* prompt the development of Darwinistic evolution. Darwin was well versed in Christian doctrines and had attended a Christian college to train for ministry.[6] However, he passionately rejected a certain doctrine—*responsibility*. To Darwin the responsibilities outlined in reliable ancient Scripture were unreasonable. He thought of evil as if it were a simple misunderstanding, and, as a result, resented the consequences that evil brings. Absolute consequences fit absolute determination. Darwin could not accept this infinite degree of justice. He confessed, "I can indeed hardly see how anyone ought to wish Christianity to be true; for if so the plain language of the text seems to show that the men who do not believe, and this would include my Father, Brother, and almost all my friends, will be everlastingly punished. And this is a damnable doctrine."[7]

When we are spiritually convicted about our wrongdoing, each of us approaches a watershed—a defining moment. If we accept the raw truth about our actions, we feel vulnerable and in need of help. It is possible, however, to *redefine* our actions internally, to convince ourselves mechanically—in conflict with the conscience. People try to deceive themselves.[a]

---

[a] 1 John 1:8

Actively denying the very existence of the *Record Keeper* reigns as the most extreme case of this form of self-deception. Reliable ancient Scripture reveals that "The fool hath *said* in his heart, There is no God"[a] (emphasis added). No one is *born* ignorant of God. No one just *happens* to be an unbeliever; it takes work! Richard Dawkins is one of the most influential and internationally acclaimed atheists of our time. He testifies, "I could not imagine being an atheist at any time before 1859, when Darwin's *Origin of Species* was published."[8] Dawkins has given an ungodly number of hours laboring to market secular concepts of evolution. He *is* an avid storyteller.[9] But, the truth will not adapt to preferences, even for the most diligent storytellers.

In Darwin's time, the struggle to reject truth was a much more difficult task. According to Mayr,[p13] "Nearly all leading naturalists of his time were ordained ministers."[10] If two of Charles Darwin's family members and several of his friends were atheists, that is quite an indictment against them. They had to work much harder to destroy their spiritual potential than we who are submersed in 21st century secularism. Given these conditions, it appears reasonably evident that Darwin literally *hated* the idea of justice.[11]

Darwin was content to redefine our world as a cold, hope-sponging machine that is equally cruel to everything that breathes. If molesting *everyone's* hope could blur the individual burden of responsibility lingering with those who refused to come clean, Darwin was game. In Darwin's mind, poisoning *hope in general* was an acceptable alternative to identifying those particular individuals who have

---

[a] Psalm 14:1; 53:1

intentionally rejected hope. The real goal of evolution has never been to assess scientific data accurately. Blurring the lines of personal responsibility was Darwin's greatest aspiration for evolution. To date, he has succeeded.

Redefining evil has become a way of life.[a] Hellish crime is bootlegging for "business as usual." Even the anti-religion secularist Harris[p19] bemoans the current state of affairs. "Child pornography alone—which, as many have noted, is the visual record of an actual crime—is now a global, multibillion-dollar industry."[12] He continues: "Apparently, there are enough people who are eager to see children—and, increasingly, toddlers and infants ... tortured so as to create an entire subculture."[13] That's evil!

"Is it?" Darwin's concept asks.

Harris and a remnant of other functionally cognizant psychologists have been spinning their wheels ferociously to prove that evil *is* real. Sadly, though, even most of these psychologists do not make the connection. They are finding out—the hard way—that they don't like Darwin's game! Denial has become a *science*. Where do we go from here? Reliable ancient Scripture awaits a sweeping rediscovery. It seems we are turning over every possible stone before we return to the Rock of Ages. The truth towers so *unmistakably* close. What drives such highly intelligent people as Harris to reject it? He represents an ungodly portion of gifted minds that have been battered mercilessly. In that, instead of benefiting from the moral concrete of reliable ancient Scripture, Harris is determined to keep bouncing his head against it.[b]

---

[a] Isaiah 5:20
[b] 2 Corinthians 4:4

He relentlessly challenges the moral Bedrock that was entrusted to our ancestors. Harris alleges that the *Author* of life is morally incompetent:

> The Creator of the Universe Himself has told us not to spare the rod, lest we spoil the child (Proverbs 13:24, 20:30, and 23:13–14). However, if we are actually concerned about human well-being, and would treat children in such a way as to promote it, we might wonder whether it is generally wise to subject little boys and girls to pain, terror, and public humiliation as a means of encouraging their cognitive and emotional development.[14]

Is the rod equivalent to public humiliation or terror? Not in my experience. Public humiliation reeks of ungodly desperation; it is *not* the natural product of corporal punishment. Public humiliation is the product of frustrated teachers and parents who have *not* used corporal punishment. Strong *private* discipline refreshes the soul with unmatched clarity and focus—not terror or humiliation. *That* is the imperative of reliable ancient Scripture. It is fact: Pain gets our cognitive and emotional juices going a whole lot better than the traditional nap in detention ever could. If we weigh the unpleasant vapor of pain (discipline) against the benefits of life lessons, the cost is literally irrelevant.

Like everything else in life, however, corporal punishment *can* be corrupted. A parent or teacher who lacks critical respect for a young person should *never* be allowed to physically discipline that child. Harris blurs the lines here. "All the research indicates that corporal punishment is a disastrous practice, leading to more violence and social pathology."[15] It sounds like someone researched the results of a psychopath beating kids. Do psychopaths make better parents when they just verbally abuse children? Physical contact gets a child's attention, and as a result the *motive* of the one using punitive contact is amplified. A disciplinary paddle is simply a megaphone to communicate a message. It works—whether the message is seasoned, godly wisdom or senseless, evil pathology. And it is certainly illogical to discard equipment because of a message that it has conveyed?

Tools are most effective when handled competently. In this case, reprimand must be tempered with care. Parents ought to *tell* their children that they love them several times throughout the day. If parents hope to make a positive impact when they discipline, their children need to know that they are cared for deeply. There is absolutely nothing kind or responsible about letting children run riot. Permissive parenting, in fact, is associated with the very types of social disorder rampant in our society—including poor impulse control, disregard for authority, low levels of self-reliance, and high levels of aggression. Further, letting a child stare down a time-out corner for the better part of a childhood is hardly a sensible alternative. This stuff is *freshman-level* life management. Fertilize and water the garden, but *pull* the weeds.

Is authoritative, or strong, discipline really unscientific? Later Harris discusses some of the causes of mental disorders. "Most important, psychopaths do not experience a normal range of anxiety and fear, and this may account for their lack of conscience."[16] Reliable ancient Scripture tells us that a reasonable degree of *fear* should curb wrongdoing.[a] Isn't strong discipline a necessary alert system?

---

[a] Job 28:28; Proverbs 3:7, 16:6

Consider Harris' statement in the same book in which he mistakenly criticizes corporal punishment.

> The first neuroimaging experiment done on psychopaths found that, when compared to nonpsychopathic criminals and noncriminal controls, they exhibit significantly less activity in regions of the brain that generally respond to emotional stimuli. While anxiety and fear are emotions that most of us would prefer to live without, they serve as anchors to social and moral norms. Without an ability to feel anxious about one's own transgressions, real or imagined, norms become nothing more than "rules that others make up." The development literature also supports this interpretation: fearful children have been shown to display greater moral understanding. It remains an open question, therefore, just how free of anxiety we can reasonably want to be.[17]

Fear gets us started off morally.[a] This strongly implies that the proper use of firm discipline is the most reasonable means of establishing sound moral values. How does a man of Harris' intelligence miss this natural inference?

Those who deny personal wrongdoing often have a habit of letting their children get overrun with spiritual diseases—dishonesty, irresponsibility, disrespect, arrogance and so on.[b] By failing to take responsibility for spiritually tattered areas in their own lives, adults stay ill-equipped to *identify* harmful vices in a second generation. Also, by failing

---

[a] Psalm 36:1, 111:10; Proverbs 1:7, 8:13, 9:10
[b] 2 Kings 17:17; Ezekiel 23:37; John 8:44

to take blame on a personal level, the parent impairs the sense of *authority* that he or she ought to maintain. *This* is the underlying reason that adults neglect their parental duties.[a] The rising generations need to be weeded, pruned, and cared for. They need a strong hand and a kind word. Psychologists who encourage parents to slack on discipline are helping no one—not the individual and not the society of which he is a member. Such counsel exposes a dire case of irresponsibility that distresses a foundational phase of life.

Abortion, the destruction of unborn babies, is similar to the neglect of strong discipline, in that both are driven by a chronic and widespread case of irresponsibility. Many parents are willing to literally murder their own children in order to avoid taking responsibility for them. None of us will ever know the potential of those silenced voices;[b] but we do know that—by almost anyone's standard—every person who has ever lived is a descendent of *one* first human couple. The defense of legalized infant murder is vividly nauseating. While emphasizing the very thing that it destroys—choice—the pro-abortion crusade expresses a distinct *lack* of regard for the choice of those who need a voice most desperately.

The same irresponsible attitude that slaughters the unborn has nestled deep into current science. The immoral *cause* of Darwin's concept has also become the common thread that *binds* it to modern textbooks and scientific journals. Irresponsibility has become the very heartbeat of many 21st century Darwinists. The reckless current follows naturally from Darwin's laissez-faire approach to evil, justice, and the truth. The whole premise of his concept hinges on a

---

[a] Proverbs 11:16; 28:13; 29:15
[b] Jeremiah 1:5; Luke 1:15

long series of mistakes that just happen to work. In Darwin's mind no one ever needed to step up and take charge. His concept embodies scientific *welfare*.

Multitudes of powerfully gifted minds now live on Darwin's crowded couch—perfectly satisfied to receive a steady stream of handouts. Behe[p24] exposes the concept's irresponsible mooching. "A gene for a protein might be duplicated by a random mutation but it does not just 'happen' to also have sophisticated new properties."[18] Nature's probability allowance has no provision for such lavish freeloading. An ungodly number of biologists have accrued overdraft checks and balances that are being ignored. Dembski[p24] audits this branch of the scientific community. "Evolutionary biology is now a field where imagination runs riot and substitutes for rigor."[19]

Nature puts a premium on diligence and consistency. Complex systems do *not* appreciate errors. If a single puzzle piece gets misplaced, it generates noteworthy irritation. But when applied to biology, this rule is amplified to a colossal n^{th} power. After describing the fabulously complex chain of action involved in blood clotting, Behe concludes: "The formation, limitation, strengthening, and removal of a blood clot is an integrated biological system."[20] An impressive array of proteins that are used in blood clotting constantly slosh together throughout the vascular system. These proteins remain largely inactive, however, until triggered by highly dependable cues. With just a tiny imbalance, the protein sequence can be triggered accidentally. The blood clot that would result could cause a stroke capable of destroying a multi-trillion-cell organism.

With every cycle of the heart, our crimson blood rushes through our arteries with a fresh supply of oxygen and nourishment for the body. Blood is decisively essential to—practically synonymous with—conscious life.[a] And yet even a minute clot can cause deadly results when its formation is accidental. The very *fabric* of life abhors error.

Much of the scientific community has rejected the message that nature operates with an intensely *deliberate* precision. Thus, instead of recognizing the connection, a few scientists have actually labored to build a case against conscious minds in *general*.

As secular psychology tightens its grip, the teeth of irresponsibility attempt to tear into the very substance of who we are. *We* are being redefined as natural force. Harris[p19] reasons: "All of our behavior can be traced to biological events about which we have no conscious knowledge: this has always suggested that free will is an illusion."[21] When people are reduced to chemical interactions, there is no one—no person—to reason *with*. There is not even a willful *reason* to discuss why or how a person behaves as he does, because behavior is just a meaningless series of events. We needn't be distressed by Harris' offensive reasoning, however, because it is not logical.

Most of us are capable of competently operating a vehicle with little or no *technical* knowledge about it (or the intricate details of how a combustion engine works). Does anyone fully understand the atomic structure of *anything* they work with? The brain is a vehicle of the soul. Exactly *how* the brain with its 100 billion-plus neurons functions, we don't know. But that doesn't stop us from using it.

Denying free will must rank among the dirtiest lies ever to slink from the pit. From that lie every foul vice

---

[a] Leviticus 17:11

imaginable ambushes its "helpless" victims. "Freely" is the first word that evil strangles.[a] Personal responsibility would logically dissolve in the absence of free will. Unless we make choices *on purpose*, we have no reason to feel responsible. We may feel uncomfortable with the consequences of our action, but we would never be able to feel legitimately responsible. Harris notes that the United States Supreme Court recognizes free will as the "universal and persistent" philosophical basis of American law.[22] What else does a system of law have to work with? Are courts to try and convict the "biological events about which we have no conscious knowledge" that Harris believes determines our behavior? Or is the goal to do away with holding anyone responsible for anything?

A functional society depends on individuals who take responsibility. Without personal responsibility everything would break down. In such a scenario we would never be able to build enough psychiatric wards and, if sufficient wards were available, we would have no responsible staff to *run* them.

---

[a] Genesis 2:16; 3:1

NEGLIGENCE

Negligence leaves low-hanging fruit to fall and rot. The greatest things in life are free and generally *ignored*. As technology advances, simple pleasures have encountered a mishmash of aggressive distractions. Although we may forget it from time to time, taking a moment to sniff the roses is entirely acceptable. Each day is a gift, and we need to pay *attention* to the opportunities that we are granted.[a] Many of the deepest insights about our world dangle well within reach. Sadly, though, it seems the average soul is too busy, too preoccupied to grasp them.

Reliable ancient Scripture gives us a key to understanding the most important aspects of life. We need to "become as little children" lest we miss the message.[b] That may seem much quite undignified for the mechanically educated soul, but it works! Kids sponge up everything they see; they *appreciate* little things that adults tend to overlook. And, as a result of *interest*, youngsters reap much better returns on their small ventures. The common mental cord that straps down all unbelievers is *ingratitude*. Ingratitude is the spiritual and intellectual equivalent of financial depreciation. Vast areas of our planet still lay unexplored by human eyes, and yet multitudes of adults feel unintrigued by the *universe*. We need a fresh sense of wonder. We need to appreciate what we *have* before us.

Like parched souls hallucinating a mirage in the desert, many atheists have neglected the water of the Word. To this day, many fiercely beat the air while imagining some awful

---
[a] Psalm 39:3
[b] Matthew 18:3

daydream. Some who refuse the Word have taken upon themselves to market everything from minor mix-ups to absurd falsehoods as though they were teachings of Scripture. And it is often a lack of appreciation that lurks at the bottom of these allegations. *Neglect* of the Word has allowed for widespread misunderstanding of the Word. Most of those who hate the "Book" actually have no idea what it is that they hate. Because of their lack of appreciation, spiritually-impoverished souls find little value in anything. Thus, they are apt to hate a thing even when they have only little knowledge about it.

In his book *Denying Evolution*, Pigliucci[p11] attacks the authority of the ancient Record. He argues that "obsession with using the Bible as a book of factual truths about the universe as opposed to spiritual insights marred the history of Western religion throughout the Middle Ages and Renaissance."[23] He is wrong, of course, for throughout recorded history people have been counterfeiting the Truth. The "facts" that marred human history during the Middle Ages were not drawn from the Well of truth. They were human inventions that got passed off using a forged stamp of divine approval. They are *not* in the Book!

The Dark Ages were dark primarily because of a *lack* of Scripture.[a24] Before the printing press, common people lacked biblical knowledge. For many years the Word was scarce. To make matters worse, the corrupt leaders of dominant medieval religion (Roman Catholicism) hid the Truth from the lay person. They intentionally kept the Word in an uncommon language so that the "church" could leverage its resources unchecked. The religious system outright *taught* its subjects

---

[a] Hosea 4:6

never to question the priest's and ultimately the Pope's final authority.

When American colonists began educating their children, this spiritual darkness is what they feared most. Early Americans recognized that spiritual darkness was the *greatest* threat associated with illiteracy. For this reason they made provision for schools and worked diligently to learn the *facts* of Scripture.[a] The power of Scripture is in the facts that it teaches. Without an understanding of facts—especially biblical facts—the spiritual import of those facts can never be grasped.[b] In his book *Why Johnny Can't Tell Right From Wrong*, William Kilpatrick reasons, "When educators neglect specific content in favor of critical thinking skills ... critical thinking itself will be one of the first casualties. A youngster won't learn to think critically if he doesn't have something to think about." [25]

Although reliable ancient Scripture primarily teaches *spiritual* principles that are light-years beyond raw scientific and historical data, all the data recorded in Scripture is flawless.[c] Casting doubt on the historical or scientific facts in Scripture is an attempt to *degrade* it—in effect calling it the word of *men*. Of course, time will tell what sincere believers have known for ages—that the very breath of *God* is written for us to read.[d] We should take care not to neglect it.

Yet, Pigliucci expresses no semblance of due respect. He has neglected to study the Word and then takes the liberty to put words in the mouth of his Creator. In his willful

---

[a] 2 Timothy 2:15; Acts 17:11
[b] Psalm 111:10; Psalm 119:34; Psalm 119:130; Proverbs 9:10
[c] Psalm 119:98–100
[d] 2 Timothy 3:16

ignorance Pigliucci shamelessly muddles reliable ancient Scripture. He says that the Scripture teaches that the earth is flat and that the earth is a stationary center of the universe. He bases these claims on passages of Scripture that say no such thing.

Pigliucci lists two references as makeshift proof of a flat-earth concept taught in the Bible.[26] Both passages refer to *spiritual* visions, and both passages refer to worldwide issues. In one passage Satan *shows* the Lord Jesus all the civilizations of the world "in a moment of time."[a] In the other passage a Babylonian king, Nebuchadnezzar, experiences a prophetic *dream*. *Three times* in the passage Nebuchadnezzar clarifies that what he saw were "visions" of his "head" while in his "bed."[b] Could he have been any more specific? These passages say *nothing* about a geologically flat earth.

With just a little more study of the Word, however, Pigliucci could have found biblical passages that *do have* something to say about the flat-earth concept. For example, the Word tells us that our Creator "hangeth the earth upon nothing."[c] Centuries of flat-earthers must have scratched their head when they came to that one ... suspended in space ... how could that be? This passage is found in the book of Job, which according to historians is one of the *oldest* books in the Scripture.

If he had continued his search, Pigliucci might have stumbled across Isaiah 40:22. In that passage we find mention of "the circle of the earth." When the book of Isaiah was written in the early part of 7th century B.C., the rounded

---

[a] Luke 4:5
[b] Daniel 4:5, 10, 13
[c] Job 26:7

shape of the earth was not yet established scientifically. Even in the late 15th century A.D. when Christopher Columbus set out for the New World, science did not know the earth was round—but Columbus did. He said, "The execution of the voyage ... is simply the fulfillment of what Isaiah had prophesied."[27] Christopher Columbus raised support, rounded up a crew, and set sail with confidence in the truth of Isaiah 40:22. He was not disappointed.

Because he neglected to study the Bible Pigliucci also alleges that Scripture presents the earth as a fixed center of the universe.[28] His patchwork proof for this accusation is Joshua 10:12–14. That passage records an event that is truly remarkable. The Scripture testifies that "there was no day like that before it or after it." On that day the nation of Israel was engaged in hand-to-hand combat with *five* Amorite nations. The Jews were so successful that Joshua, the commander of the Israeli forces, prayed for a longer day. And it happened. The sun and moon both stopped their apparent motion until the conflict was settled. For nearly 24 hours celestial objects were frozen in space. Whether God stopped the rotation of the Milky Way Galaxy or the expansion of the entire universe, there was a definite celestial pause.

The events recorded in this passage are certainly awesome and unique, but what do they imply about physics between the sun and the earth? Joshua wanted the sun to stay a while. He prayed for that, and the Master worked out the details. But it is simply not realistic to classify everyone who uses the term "sunrise" or "sunset" as a geocentrist. And it is not realistic to classify the Scripture as a document that teaches geocentricity on the basis of passages that refer to the rising and the setting of the sun. Rather, the whole canon of Scripture is given *to* human beings to be understood *by* human beings. In this world people see a sun that peeks over the horizon in the morning and dips off the other side at night. It is just how we live. That is our perspective.

For instance, does the Bible also misrepresent the properties of electromagnetic waves when it references the color of various objects? The Gospel of Mark makes the observation that the grass where Jesus taught was *green*.[a] But that could be considered unscientific. Just ask any informed 21st-century scientist. Grass is not really green—it just appears green to the ignorant masses. Grass appears green because the chlorophyll in its blades reflects the green electromagnetic wavelength. The reflected green light is detected by the human eye. For that reason, we are all *duped* into believing that grass is green.

Maybe grass is just supposed to look green. For whatever reason, the most informed 21st-century scientists still feel comfortable calling colors like they see them. And they also calculate the expected time of "sunrise" and "sunset" for our daily newspaper. The terms are practical, clear, and effective.

With a little more study of the Word, Pigliucci could have found biblical passages that have something to say about geocentricity as well. Psalm 19:4 tells us that in space the Creator "set a tabernacle for the sun." A tabernacle is a structure that is set in a fixed location. Again, this could have made for some frankly puzzled geocentrists over the centuries. The sun has a specific position in space? Why does it seem as though it is circling us every day? But even when it is difficult

---

[a] Mark 6:39

to fully understand, the Scripture always stays well ahead of the times.

Everybody believes in something. When we neglect the reading of Truth, our belief systems can grow sketchy. The idea that atheism is not a religion is one of the most deceptive concepts embedded in our culture. Whether or not they admit it, atheists believe in God—they believe they *are* God with respect to their basis of faith. That is, the atheist believes that human intellect is the final Word of life. Atheism was the first alternate religious system. It outdates Islam, Buddhism, Greek mythology, and every misguided religion. Atheism is no exception to the rule; it is a *spiritual* condition.

When secularists propagate their doctrine to the upcoming generations, they often insist that their belief system is scientific. It is *not*. The First Amendment was supposed to protect us from religious monopolies, and yet Darwinism and the like have slipped under the radar by masquerading as science and not a belief system. Public classrooms have often become Darwinistic church services. Truth is not welcome. It's not that other concepts compete for class time; secularism is increasingly preached as the *official* state religion—exactly what the First Amendment was written to protect *against*. Pigliucci attempts to justify the violation claiming because "creationism is a religion and [Darwinian] evolution is not, the teaching of the former is prohibited in public schools, while that of the latter is protected."[29] Really?

We've come a long way since the "Old Deluder Satan Act." Society has been duped and we are missing the *real* evil that is at work. The Scopes "monkey" trial of 1925 ended with a ruling *against* teaching Darwinism in American public classrooms. In just 94 years we have turned the tables 180 degrees. In the modern public biology curriculum we often find little *but* Darwinism. America has lost her footing, and she is slipping deeper and deeper into a pit of spiritual incompetence.

America needs to find her *base* and gain traction. If she hopes to reverse the trend and make legitimate progress, there is no other option. America is defined by her citizens; and so, we must—as individuals—flesh out meaningful beliefs. We need a revolution of personal integrity. *That* will lead us to the answers found in reliable ancient Scripture. The original groundwork of the United States will still support our weight just fine—*if* we stay on it.

The toxic venom that certain godless members of our modern scientific community inject into the veins of society is often a direct product of negligence. Secularists have lost their blush. The Truth is available today every bit as much as it ever has been, but it provides no help if it is neglected. Truth—like cash behind the dryer—never loses its value. But what *help* is truth if we never let it see the light of day? As one more generation picks at reheated bones, the Fortune of truth glimmers in a nearby corner collecting lint.

Is it any wonder that the pieces of life don't seem to fit together after we have pitched the Instruction Manual? Through neglect of the Scripture, Darwinism rallied an ungodly number of supporters and planted its first roots. Mayr[p13] recounts the event. "A closer study of living nature ... revealed an alarming amount of brutality and waste. As scientists came to understand more and more about the natural world, the credibility of perfect design by a benign creator further declined."[30] One of the early symptoms of a truth deficiency is rose-colored glasses—playing naïve about the real and devastating consequences of evil.[a]

Reliable ancient Scripture describes the current natural world as a *corrupted* environment.[b] It exclaims that all of nature *groans* in "pain"[c] as a result of our sin. To be quite frank, *none* of us likes that burden of responsibility. It follows then that as the Truth slips from our hands, the reality of sin and its consequences are the first things we forget. Natural scientists should have *expected* to find widespread violence and decay consistent with the causes revealed in Scripture. Observation parallels the written Truth with frightening precision. Nature displays an immense and divinely sophisticated beauty, but it is tainted! Our world is messed up—and the Book explains why.

The concrete moral guidance of Scripture lends a refreshing stability to our lives. It teaches us how we ought to live and leads us to the One who can walk us through the necessary steps. Like gravity, moral laws restrict us. They keep our feet on the ground. To build a stable life we *need* this moral bedrock to serve as a firm foundation. We are made "in the image of God,"[d] and because of that a certain part of us has a desire for moral truth. It is a human need.

Harris[p19] cites relevant research. "While having *some* choice is generally good, it seems that having too many options tends to undermine our feelings of satisfaction, no matter which option we choose. Knowing this, it could be rational to strategically limit one's choices."[31] We are built for

---

[a] Isaiah 48:22
[b] Genesis 3:14-19
[c] Romans 8:22
[d] Genesis 9:6

freedom within limits. Choosing to stay within moral limits is a distinctive of God's image.

Although it seems as though right and wrong should be common sense, in real-life situations people are not honest enough with themselves.... "The heart is deceitful."[a] For that reason we need to adopt moral laws that are set in stone.[b] We need to agree to moral boundaries before we get immersed in a situation, before lines get blurred.

The need for solid moral answers grows more apparent by the day. Harris believes that human cultures will ultimately develop common standards of morality.[32] This naturally implies that we should expect a universal moral code that is yet awaiting discovery ... or perhaps *recognition*. So—in Harris' mind—the jury is still out, whereas believers have found the verdict *passed*.

There is nothing to deliberate about; the Truth stands written albeit too little *read*. The development of new technologies is not our greatest prospect. We need to use what we *have* properly.[c]

---

[a] Jerermiah 17:9
[b] Exodus 24:12; 31:18; 34:1 ; Deuteronomy 4:13; 5:22
[c] 1 Timothy 6:6

DISRESPECT

Light enters the eye. Passing through a thin protective layer, it meets a second curved surface. This second layer, the cornea, gently bends the light photons toward a critical point. Once behind the cornea, the photons slide smoothly through a narrow pocket of crystal-clear fluid, on track for their destination. The light approaches a shrewd gateway. Only a specified percentage of the photons are permitted beyond this checkpoint.

Those that make the cut find themselves barreling into an actively flexing surface—the lens. Because the lens is composed of an elastic, transparent material, photons are commonly directed with ease and precision. After passing through all the crystal seams of the lens, the light is finally on its ultimate course. It glides through a soft glassy substance as it makes its way to the back of a large rounded cavity. *That* is where vision starts.

Each of the millions of photons strikes a specialized cell. These specialized cells have two primary categories: cone cells that detect color and rod cells that detect trace intensities of light. By converting the physical properties of the photons into nerve impulses, the *millions* of cone and rod cells transmit messages into the optic nerves. Of these receptor cells, all those on the nose side of each eye send their data to the opposite side of the head. The optic nerves that carry that half of the data crisscross behind the nose. And, in this way, the brain receives the combined information from the left and the combined information from the right, bundled respectively. When the brain receives the neatly packaged information, only a vanishingly small fraction of a second has passed since the photons first made contact with the eye. But what's to see?

Respect, by definition, demands a second look. We have lost the art of wonder. If life seems dull and predictable, it is only because *we* have become dull and predictable. There is something enormously sophisticated about being dumbstruck from time to time. The patterns of nature are far too breathtaking to leave us unmoved.

At a distance of about 93 million miles from the nearest star, our planet zips around its orbit at roughly 66,000 miles per hour ... all day, every day. That means that at any given moment we are moving at a minimum velocity of 66,000 miles per hour. If the 580-million-mile path that the earth treks each year could be illustrated by the circumference of a two-millimeter copper pellet, our *galaxy* would stretch a little farther than the borders of North America in comparison. We have no idea how to realistically grapple with that kind of information. There are over 200 billion galaxies in the universe, which means you could observe 1 new *galaxy* per second nonstop for well over 6,000 years. Scientists who profess to have a *mastery* of such things have lost touch with reality. To say that we have the tip of an iceberg is too generous. We have not even exposed much of a *tip*.

All the way from this cosmic level, disrespect trickles down into even the most common relationships. The upcoming generation has learned little about respect. Employers must work hard to find respectful employees. Respect for teachers, for government officials, for peers, for fellow human beings ... respect even for parents has grown scarce. This harvest of disrespect has sprouted from deeply-planted philosophical seeds.

Humanistic philosophy is all about downgrading the natural world. In order to inflate the human ego, humanism—whether outright or not—plays down all the marvels of nature. Humanism makes fanciful claims that even science wouldn't dare touch. For instance, Pigliucci[p6] claims that the pieces of our cosmos don't fit together as well as they should. To prop this opinion he says, "It often takes quite a bit of imagination to see any purpose in some aspects of the universe."[33] Because *he* doesn't understand it, the universe is flawed. Really? What happened to good old-fashioned wonder?

Dawkins[p10] lacks respect as well. He shamelessly bashes the whole field of physics with several nasty backhanded remarks. In his book *The Blind Watchmaker*, Dawkins presumes, "Physics is the study of simple things that do not tempt us to invoke design."[34] Maybe the rest of the world are just dullards. Physics ... simple? Don't feel bad; Dawkins later clarifies that he is speaking from a general lack of respect. "Even large physical objects like stars consist of a rather limited array of parts, more or less *haphazardly* arranged"[35] (emphasis added). How can he be so sure—since no one has ever actually visited a star, and the atomic structure of stars is a subject of continuing scientific discussion? As a general rule, the field of physics shows that matter is anything *but* haphazard.

Well, at least Dawkins has nominal respect for his own field (biology). He makes an awesome point. "The objects and phenomena that a physics book describes are simpler than a single cell in the body of its author."[36] He also points out that the processes that take place inside of cells are beyond our current mathematical models.[37] This means that living cells are too complex for us to do the math. That is some seriously wonderful complexity.

Later in his book, however, even *this* air of respect gets polluted. Although he provides an impressive picture, Dawkins does not really grasp the immense weight of this complexity. He proposes that the cell sprang into existence as a freak accident.[38] He actually believes that this is mathematically conceivable. Dawkins likens the odds of spontaneous generation to the odds of randomly shuffling a couple decks of 52 cards back into the factory order.[39] Where went that respect?

Given the precise structure of discrete elements within the nucleotides, any real cell contains specific complexity comparable—at least—to the full text of *Encyclopedia Britannica*.[40] To form a cell randomly is analogous to writing *Encyclopedia Britannica* by randomly shuffling letters, numbers, punctuation marks, and spaces. That probability would be far less likely than 1 in $10^{294,000,000}$ if we were to ignore all but the letters.[41] That means that if there were $10^{293,000,000}$ universes like ours, and if there were a hundred trillion events per atom per second, and there were a trillion years in each universe, a random event such as this occurring in any one of those universes would be categorically impossible.[42] Although a living cell is far more complex than an encyclopedia, this comparison reveals the shameless level of disrespect Darwinists employ.

Without respect we get disoriented. Kilpatrick[p49] has researched the role of respect as it relates to the development of an individual's worldview. He has found that personal achievement is driven by an aspiration to imitate *heroes*.[43] When a person develops an overall lack of respect, he loses his footing. Without respect we begin to tumble aimlessly through life. Our surroundings can poke and prod us along, but we cannot thrive in such a manner. Somewhere along the way we need to take initiative. Having a working system of *respect* allows us to move forward with purpose and confidence. Without such a system, we are tossed like jellyfish by every whim of our environment.

Reliable ancient Scripture drives at the importance of respect with striking vigor. Respect for the *Creator* reigns as one of the grandest themes of all time. The word "holy" indicates wholeness. As the *Author* of all things proper, God's personal traits *define* the final standard of conduct.[a] He is "holy, holy, holy."[b] To orient ourselves in this world, a firm grasp of His holiness is indispensable. All things are relative to *it*. Divine holiness provides us with a flawless, universal model. We must, by all rights, pay close attention. God's *essence* demands respect!

If, however, we focus heavily on ourselves rather than divine holiness, we will wander senselessly—trying to make sense of our nonsense *using* our own nonsense. This again is the goal of consequentialism. Consequentialism argues that moral truth can be established by human logic (rationalizing)—in effect reinventing the wheel. This teaching is based on a rude desire to discredit the Author of morality. One of the

---

[a] Leviticus 19:2; Isaiah 48:17
[b] Isaiah 6:3; Revelation 4:8

early symptoms of self-absorption is an insatiable thirst to degrade others, especially our Creator.

Harris[p19] claims—with no semblance of shame—that our *personal* well-being should carry infinitely more value than our Maker's standards. He asks brashly, "What would our world be like if we ceased to worry about 'right' and 'wrong,' or 'good' and 'evil,' and simply acted so as to maximize well-being, our own and that of others? Would we lose anything important?"[44] To answer his reckless question: We would lose *much*—including our well-being. To clarify his point, Harris is implying that we should violate our conscience for what we *think* will work. But, the conscience is the most powerful faculty that the human mind uses to determine right and wrong. Can a farmer maximize his productivity without powered equipment?

To seek the greatest possible well-being of the masses without respect for right and wrong is a contradiction of terms. But *more* importantly, by attempting to reinvent the conscience mechanically, we would be discarding the God-given truth that we have. *That* is starkest hazard of following through with Harris' suggestion. It pulls down the road signs that point to the fount of all things good—the lodestar that is our Creator's holiness.

Harris is *aggressively* shameless in his disrespect for his Maker. He forces the point. "If the difference between the Bad Life and the Good Life doesn't matter to a person, what could possibly matter to him? Is it conceivable that something might matter *more* than this difference, expressed on the widest possible scale?"[45] The good life matters to a *degree*, but the purposes of the *Creator* carry incomparably more weight than our little über-isolated ideas of success from day to day. Harris tries to cover his argument by throwing in a provision for the "widest scale," but all his ideas must logically bubble down to *individual* opinions as to what the "Good Life" is. He leaves no provision for discovering the Good Life in terms of its Inventor.

Life and good are not ours to create. They are paid-for gifts that come with a complete Instruction Manual and personal Guide.[a] The thoughts of the Creator broaden the scope of our opinion to an unparalleled degree. If we neglect to show respect for divine wisdom, we will fritter away our time searching for moral principles that are literally close enough to trip over. They are readily available in our generation, printed in a bound Text. Disrespect dulls and disorganizes keen minds, and as a result, much energy is spent for no good reason. If the garage is too cluttered to find our car, we need to have more respect for our stuff—*not* finance a replacement vehicle.

A life rooted in disrespect is bound for hurt. Harris apparently recognizes nothing beyond this type of existence. He comments:

> Religious people are as eager to find happiness and to avoid misery as anyone else.... And while Judaism is sometimes held up as an exception—because it tends not to focus on the afterlife—the Hebrew Bible makes it absolutely clear that Jews should follow Yahweh's law *out of concern for the negative consequences of not following it.*[46]

---

[a] James 1:17

We are commanded to honor God out of *love* for Him.[a] And in this honor we ought to follow the other commandments. Negative consequences serve as street signs to orient our attention toward truth. They are a teaching tool, *not* a final motivator.[b] If our children never grow beyond consequences … if they never develop a relationship with us, we can be confident that our time with them has been a wretched failure.

Voluntary respect does a much finer job than force at adding weight to words. Many of the scientific arguments that atheists make are fueled by a lack of respect toward their Creator. They cannot move forward because they do not trust the Word that they have been given. Consider Harris' statement:

> Here is our situation: if the basic claims of religion are true, the scientific worldview is so blinkered and susceptible to supernatural modification as to be rendered nearly ridiculous; if the basic claims of religion are false, most people are profoundly confused about the nature of reality, confounded by irrational hopes and fears, and tending to waste precious time and attention—often with tragic results. Is this really a dichotomy about which science can claim to be neutral?[47]

The real issue is that atheists disrespect the Word of God. To an atheist, scientific laws all just *happen* to work for now. The believer has a treasure chest of promises that the atheist does

---

[a] Deuteronomy 6:5; 11:1; 13:1; Joshua 22:5; 23:11; Proverbs 3:9; Matthew 22:37–37; Mark 12:30; Luke 10:27; John 8:42
[b] Galatians 3:24–25, Hebrews 12:6–7

not. Whose natural worldview is "blinkered and susceptible"? The Book that believers use says, "The Eternal God is thy refuge."[a] It guarantees, "I am the Lord, I change not."[b] In contrast, the secular books all rest on a scattered assortment of so-far-so-good notes. Believers stand on the sound integrity of Almighty God to maintain the dependability of the natural laws. The secular *just-cuz* worldview is *not* more secure than the Eternal God—but forever less secure, for God *invented* natural consistency.

Darwinism is a mockery of science. It assumes that all the complexity of the natural world just happened. Natural selection proposes that nature has a keen eye for picking out good *mistakes*. That means that our natural world and all the things living in it have been degraded shamelessly by the concept. Darwinists are perfectly comfortable with calling nature a pile of mistakes.

If a single cell represents more information than physics books, how does anyone get off calling it a mistake? There is an unmistakable issue of disrespect here. Nature does not tend to organize itself. It strongly tends toward disorder—toward entropy. This clearly implies that nature was organized by a deliberate force.

Greene[p9] illustrates the direct relationship between growing complexity and pressure toward entropy. If we were to remove the binding of *War and Peace* and throw all 1,386 pages high into the air, they would not tend to land in a neatly numbered order. He vows that "With more certainty than death and taxes, we can count on systems with many constituents *evolving* toward *disorder*"[48] (emphasis added). If

---

[a] Deuteronomy 33:27
[b] Malachi 3:6

1,386 pages are enough to make the point, where does that leave *massively* complex systems such as living cells? They are disrespected! Darwinism begins by calling the living cell an accident and only worsens from there.

Notice that Greene links evolution with *disorder*. This is not uncommon among 21st-century physicists and Darwinists. Evolution simply means *change*. It is *neutral* overall, which means that we should not be impressed with any living complexity. Darwinism downplays the wonder of life in general. For a great deal of the scientific community, respect has grown foreign.

In much the same way that Darwinism disrespects the natural world, so many people of the world have disrespected the Jews throughout recorded history. As God's chosen people, Israel has suffered more merciless criticism and harassment than any other group of people. Lindsey[p12] says this about the open contempt toward the Jewish people: "It would appear that the only way to remain a popular leader in the Arab world today is to keep the flames of hatred toward the state of Israel fanned to a fever pitch."[49] In his book *What Hath God Wrought*, William Grady discusses in great detail the dangers of disrespecting the nation of Israel.[50] Disrespect costs more than anyone can afford. The history of Israel exemplifies that truth most distinctly.

We would do well to reexamine the implications of nature and human history. We are overlooking too much. The natural world trumpets the truth of reliable ancient Scripture with high-definition clarity. If we miss the message, it is to our shame. If only cynics would look at the real world *again*, they could well get it. There is so *much* to see.

SELFISHNESS

Finally, after 40 weeks of anticipation, the moment has arrived. It's been a long road. What started with an overwhelming sense of surprise quickly developed into a battery of unusual aches and pains. Slowly the elegant outline of a lady revealed a change. Sleep often eluded her as she approached the final moments. The intensely exciting and terrifying day marched ever closer—loosely scheduled but certain. Then, when the day came, a great work was before her. She *felt* as the new life began moving from her womb. For long moments, even hours, she labored to see the infant who had spent the last months with her. Ever so gradually, the head began to crown. Until, at last, it happened. Now, for the first time, a glowing mother sees and hears this child. And, at that sacred moment, no time is lost. Between precious first cries, the baby begins smacking her little tongue against the tiny roof of her mouth. She hungers for more.

One of the greatest privileges in life is selfless giving. The beauty of a new mother is flatly unrivaled. In a unique and powerful sense, she can feel and express the wonder of having a special part in the life of another. Her love for the child can consume her in an inexpressibly graceful way. Here is an unusually good model of clean, robust love.

Although selflessness has a refreshing—almost mystical—influence on us, none of us is born selfless. In fact, from a natural point of view, *selfishness* seems much more practical. Selfishness means that we live ultimately for *ourselves*. Many scientists, philosophers, and psychologists have struggled to redefine all that we do as selfish, or motivated by self-interest. For instance: the kind gesture of a friendly neighbor is really only a means of gaining benefits later ... the commitments a bride and groom make are driven by lust and greed ... the ministry of a pastor is simply for money ... the patriotism of a soldier is really only a desire for fame or wealth ... the love of a mother is just a way of safeguarding her own genes ... and so on. The most disturbing fact about these ideas is that they *all* occur! In other words, people have the *capacity* to do all these things with selfish motives.

We should know better, however. Selfishness is reasonable, but it is immature. It *is possible* to genuinely care about others.[a] Indeed, genuine compassion for others is something that we *must* rightfully learn. Just as children should learn to walk physically, so they should also learn the moral hazards of self-centeredness. Children should learn that they are made in the image of God and that giving to others is a wonderful honor. We all have needs, but focusing too intently on those needs can be very hurtful—both to ourselves and to others.

Reliable ancient Scripture commands us to be content with what we already have and not to desire the possessions of others.[b] *Appreciation* allows us to give from our abundance.[c] Selfishness may be natural, but it is not mature, and it is not the best way to live. Our Creator enjoys giving, and He has made us with a desire to give. Selfishness forfeits the greatest opportunities and joys of living.

Darwinism operates on an extreme form of selfishness. "Survival of the fittest" is a largely advertised aspect of Darwin's concept of natural selection. Nature is painted as a

---

[a] 1 Peter 3:8; Jude 1:22
[b] Exodus 20:17; Deuteronomy 5:21; 1 Timothy 6:8; Hebrews 13:5
[c] 1 Timothy 6:6

cruel machine that kills all but the fittest. In other words, it's every plant and animal for itself ... even every *cell* for itself! That sour thought, however, turns stomachs more than it provides a working theory of the natural world.

Darwinists dream of a monumentally complex, single-celled living system suddenly popping to life. With all its millions of functional components, *one* spontaneous cell represents an exceptionally exhausting figment of the imagination. That is where all the fantastic stories of Darwinism begin. Darwinists believe that one miracle cell and billions of years created it all. But even after the miracle of spontaneous generation/abiogenesis, Darwin's creation myth runs quickly into its first dead end. Nature has no interest in bringing the individual cells together.

Nature has no need of larger organisms and will not finance the project of bringing cells together. And so, assuming the miracle cell had a way of duplicating itself and finding food, the world would soon be overrun by individual cells. In a world where survival of the fittest is the final rule, cells would *endlessly* compete with one another. So that's the story. All that imagination and we still didn't get anything bigger than a microbe.

Some Darwinists, however, believe that *selfishness* has the power to bring individual cells together in order to form larger organisms.[51] Although it is true that certain plants and animals work together, they do *not* share their genes. For instance, Spanish moss may grow on a cypress tree, but Spanish moss does not somehow grow out of cypress seeds. Scientists should know better. Yet, the concept of gene fusion between selfish cells has stuck like a weird bedtime story.

The implications of this belief are unsettling. Darwinists would have us believe that every cell of our bodies is selfish. In the Darwinist's mind, human bodies are masses of selfishness. Although this hypothetical scenario is entirely based on empty speculation, it is *not* an outlying concept. The importance of selfishness in bringing cells together has become a key tenet of secular orthodoxy and is now a belief firmly held by *mainstream* science. It has become a popular notion, notwithstanding the fact that it lacks any logical or scientific basis and is a repulsive disgrace to life in general.

Yet, we needn't bristle at the insult; a closer inspection exposes strong evidence to the contrary. Humans have a deep-seated appreciation for selflessness. We are moved with admiration by those who give for the sake of others. Jesus Christ says, "Love your enemies, bless them that curse you, do good to them that hate you, and pray for them which despitefully use you, and persecute you."[a] The words refresh the soul like time with a childhood friend. The words stir an ember of truth that tugs at our very core. As life is a *gift*, so we should give. We know, but not because Darwin has taught us.

We profoundly respect sincere kindness, but this intimate respect comes as a lethal shock to Darwinism. Mayr[p13] remarks, "It is difficult to construct a scenario in which benevolent behavior toward competitors and enemies could be rewarded by natural selection."[52] That is quite an understatement. The selfless capacities the human spirit so admires are the absolute antithesis of natural selection. The fact is so plain that it stifles even the blockbuster storytellers of Darwinism. They tend to shuffle awkwardly around the point.

---

[a] Matthew 5:44

Is it possible that humans have a unique degree of appreciation for selflessness? Research seems to suggest that we do. Human minds experience a kind of "warm glow" when thinking about genuine giving. Harris[p19] discusses this but misses the message. He concludes that "the traditional opposition between selfish and selfless motivation seems to break down. If helping others can be rewarding, rather than merely painful, it should be thought of as serving the self in another mode."[53] There is a contradiction here. If we give sincerely, we cannot be selfish; and if we give generously, we cannot expect a net gain. Giving is itself wonderful—a fact that makes little sense to an ungodly mind. Our built-in admiration for authentic kindness is a divine fingerprint.

The Master's way is perfect. We cannot find the joy of serving others until we let go of our selfishness. When we internally let go of external things, we can find the delight that our Creator has designed us to enjoy. The testimony of the Master is built right into us.... "It is more blessed to give than to receive."[a] As long as we grasp worldly philosophy, the joy of giving will forever elude us. But the pleasure is always *waiting* to be experienced because it is a neurological fact. Certainly there will be times of hurt and difficulty in the right path, but it remains an honor to know our Maker and to follow His ways. And in those times of challenge the light of His presence shines more brightly. Our first priority should always be to honor Him.

If, however, we give merely to feel our hand patting our back, our insincerity must logically reduce the degree of "warm" sensation that we feel. The person's hypocrisy will, in effect, callous and numb that person's back. Ulterior motives

---

[a] Acts 20:35

break down every natural gift. They can strip human dignity and encage us in a beastly darkness. Jesus warns, "If therefore the light that is in thee be darkness, how great is that darkness!"[a] Trying to use the benefits of godliness without having an appropriate sincerity promises a bleak end. The nearsightedness of sin blinds us to the fruitful way of faith. So that, God "hid" that good way from the self-serving.[b]

Harris does not understand the relationship. He finds that "Religious notions of morality ... are not exceptions to our common concern for well-being."[54] Paul disagrees. In the Book of Philippians, the Apostle Paul says, "I have suffered the loss of all things" and then quickly clarifies that they mean "dung" to him in comparison to his relationship with Christ.[c] Then in the Book of Romans, he tells us that he was willing to give away his own soul and his relationship with Christ for the sake of others who needed to know the Master.[d] John the Baptist also disagrees. In the Gospel of John, he tells it straight: "He must increase, but I must decrease."[e] These are only a sampling of hundreds of testimonies throughout Scripture.[f] Selfish religion may be out there, but it is *not* prescribed in the Book.

The testimonies of biblical saints resound with honor toward the Master, and at the same time they silence the ignorance of godless voices. In his book *I Don't Have Enough Faith to Be an Atheist*, Geisler points out:

---

[a] Matthew 6:23
[b] Matthew 11:25; Luke 10:21
[c] Philippians 3:8
[d] Romans 9:1–3
[e] John 3:30
[f] Isaiah 6:5

The New Testament writers had every earthly motive to *deny* the Resurrection rather than proclaim it. There was no motive or incentive to make up the New Testament storyline. The last time we checked, the promise of submission, servitude, persecution, torture, and death would not motivate anyone to make up such a story.[55]

The work of the Master does not lend itself to humanistic explanations.

Self-interest *can* motivate all we do, but it *should* not. Self-centeredness does not encourage good moral standards. In fact, selfishness makes for a very *poor* tutor of morality. Whether or not secular psychologists recognize this point, having a personal agenda necessarily taints charitable behaviors. The right motivation flows from the wonder and respect that God's essence demands. That's hard to counterfeit. When we realize who He is, we find a great Standard set and ourselves humbled—as rapt school-children—beside it.

PRIDE

November 13, 1933: Berlin is abuzz with excitement. A religious rally is in full swing at the local Sportpalast. With 20,000 in attendance, the event promises to be an unusually distinguished affair. An impressive list of highly intellectual and celebrated speakers graces the occasion, and their deft language incites surges of energy and thunderous applause. But amid the storm of activity a foul spirit is prowling the little piece of real-estate. Inside the auditorium emblems of faith and humanism mingle on their colorful banners—a symptom of the vile and terminal disease festering beneath the evening's skin-deep charm.

With seasoned arrogance the orators announce that they have professionally assessed the ancient Scripture and found it *inadequate*. It is therefore the recommendation of these scholars that the most ancient portion of the Scripture be permanently discarded. In the face of hundreds of earlier generations, they stand and proclaim that *their* Word carries greater weight than that of their Creator. In response, an ungodly portion of the event's spellbound religious audience cheers freakishly in agreement.

Pride muddies the waters of the human spirit with unmatched stealth and persistence. Pride is the most underestimated and misunderstood trait in our world. It is coddled like a friendly housecat, only to devour families and nations—as the king of all predatory beasts. Pride is *not* our friend. If we let it bed down in our soul, it *will* inevitably rip us limb from limb. It is an authentic monster and must be identified as such. It will not be tamed. It will not be domesticated. It will not rest without blood.

In recent generations pride has been defined very loosely. To clarify, pride is *not* simply self-respect or satisfaction in a job well done. Pride is the act of taking brazen liberties with or running off with another person's assets—especially assets that are entrusted to us. It is evil. If we take full credit for something that we are *gifted* enough to do, we miss the bottom line.

When we are puffed up with pride, we are in a weak, unrealistic position and thus make claims that are impossible to back up, inevitably losing our footing.[a] By accepting undue praise, people literally convince themselves that they *can* do things that they *cannot* dependably do. There is a direct relationship between how much pride people allow and how far they drift from reality. As pride increases and heads swell, people become more and more detached from reality. The higher they get on themselves, the further they have to fall when their bubble bursts.

Humility keeps us grounded as nothing else can. Noah Webster traced the word "humble" to an old Latin word *humus* meaning "earth."[56] Pride pulls us from reality. And *humility* is the only cure; it keeps our toes in the soil.

Psychologist Erik Erikson developed a very popular theory of human development based on the ego. He broke up the human lifespan into eight stages of personal development. According to Erikson every stage of our life serves to develop some specific "ego strength." We experience a series of identity crises, each of which corresponds directly to a given stage. If we pass an identity-crisis test, we develop a related strength; if we fail, on the other hand, we develop a related weak spot.[57]

---

[a] Proverbs 16:18

Although Erikson's theory defines a very real process in our lives, he left out the most essential factor. When we convince ourselves that *we* are capable of handling life's challenges on our own, we cripple ourselves. Pride handicaps us. The Scripture teaches us to find the strength that we need for life's trials in the Master.[a] He is the source of all strength and promises to give us strength in our times of need. Resting in *God's* ability and finding *Him* capable is the best way to advance through the eight stages that Erikson discovered. Our Maker *never* has an identity crisis, and we will always find Him *legitimately* competent. Without this crucial insight, our self-concept will always be built upon an unhealthy measure of unstable hot air.

The first occurrence of the word "pride" in reliable ancient Scripture offers great clarity as to its proper definition. Leviticus 26:19 introduces pride with the prepositional phrase "of your power." This phrase sheds tremendous light on the subject—revealing the powerhouse behind the monster. The more we advertise and emphasize the capabilities of *human* power, the more we fill ourselves with the hot air of pride.

If we focus too heavily on human achievement, we become blind to all that is truly great, as a dark cloud of humanism obscures the daylight of truth. In his book *Mein Kampf*, Adolf Hitler wrote:

> All that we admire in the world to-day, its science, its art, its technical developments and discoveries, are the products of the creative activities of a few peoples ... The maintenance of civilization is wholly dependent on such peoples. Should they perish, all that makes

---

[a] Matthew 6:24-34

this earth beautiful will descend with them into the grave.[58]

If we see human accomplishments as the *most* beautiful features of our environment, we are mentally sick. This relationship between pride and mental detachment is a disturbingly common condition. Pride blinds people to the import of their surroundings. Dawkins[p10] feels that "modern theologians of any sophistication have given up believing in instantaneous creation."[59] He is wrong, but he is not far from the facts. As we grow in knowledge, we have a definite tendency to grow *arrogant*.[a] Arrogance, in turn, detaches people from the truth. Thus, we find an alarming number—a *majority*—of "educated believers" who believe *nothing* of substance. If our confidence is based on what *we* have learned rather than on what has been divinely revealed, our confidence and overall impact will tend to dissolve. Unless we are grounded in humility, we will fail to carry weight in our beliefs and certainly fail to carry *enough* weight in our beliefs to care for the soul of a man like Richard Dawkins.

Pride misleads us. It may well be that Dawkins[p10] has convinced himself. But, then again, who is sounding an alarm anymore? He says, "I may not always be right, but I care passionately about what is true and I never say anything that I do not believe to be right."[60] Although he is willing to overstate his condition to make the point, as a general rule Dawkins seems to believe in the concepts he has been promoting. Pride is frightfully deceitful.[b] Who can tell the man his error?

---

[a] 1 Corinthians 8:1
[b] Jeremiah 49:16; Obadiah 1:3

Dawkins has come to hate the Scripture. In his discussion of the Cambrian explosion he admits:

> When we are talking about gaps of this magnitude... Both schools of thought [secular ways of interpreting evolution] despise so-called scientific creationists equally, and both agree ... that the only alternative explanation of the sudden appearance of so many complex animal types in the Cambrian era is divine creation, and both would reject this alternative.[61]

Secular evolution is an attempt at accounting for the origin of biological complexity by means of storytelling; it is all about imaginative power—not science. Reliable ancient Scripture is not nearly as pride-pampering as the complex stories of Darwinists. In fact, the scriptural account of creation is downright simple—often *too* simple for the "educated" soul.[a]

Dawkins has gone to extreme measures to degrade his Maker. Dawkins has proposed that God is a *human* idea that has been passed down through generations like a virus.[62] To establish the idea, he coined a term—"memes"—to refer to ideas that pass stealthily from generation to generation. Memes are Dawkins' attempt to avoid the question of timeless truths. Supposedly, common ideas and behavioral patterns flow naturally through generations—using, as it were, mindless hosts. Although his concept is logically weak, it has gained surprising attention. We *may* pass information between generations unconsciously, but the information is fairly trivial. It by no means explains our perceptions of truth.

---

[a] 1 Corinthians 1:18-31

Let's illustrate the logic here. In high school many of us used to play the telephone game. One person would tell another some "secret," and then the message would get passed one-on-one down a line of listeners. The end result was always a hilarious twisted sentence that bore faint or no resemblance to the original message. In contrast, a spiritually uneducated soul can hear the Word of God and immediately sense the scalpel of timeless truth picking out the cancers of his heart. Whereas human word of mouth dissolves through time and space, truth does not. Like the genes of that old fish coelacanth that we discussed in the previous chapter, Truth remains intact.[a]

Dawkins is not alone, however, in attacking reliable ancient Scripture. The *absolute* most fabulously disturbing activity in all of recorded history may well be modern textual criticism of the very Breath of God. *Religious* scholars have desecrated the Words of Scripture with shameless unbelief. They have taken it upon themselves to discredit the Written Word. Consider the following footnote placed inside a copy of God's Breath:

> Because the other Gospels provide such full accounts of appearances of Jesus after His resurrection, it is curious and somewhat frustrating that *Mark's writing stopped at 16:8*. Perhaps he had written more, but *his ending was lost*. The scribes who added verses 9–20 pulled from other scriptures as well as historical witnesses to the post-resurrection lives of apostles. Therefore, the events recorded here

---

[a] Psalm 117:2

are true but *not part of Mark's original record* (emphasis added).[63]

Mark 16:9–20 was never "lost." It was rejected by people who do not like the Bible's authority and who openly doubt the power of Almighty God to preserve it.

It is often noted that Nazi Germany was still religious during the time of the Holocaust. As pride—including religious pride—*burnt* God's people in that day, so textual critics butcher God's Word in our day. As the breath was snuffed from the people of God in that day, so the very Breath of God is muffled in our day. The Word of God is being mutilated and redefined with ungodly brashness.

The King James Bible *is* reliable ancient Scripture. It has been purified seven times.[a] It was translated with more linguistic competence and textual resources than the world will ever know again. But infinitely more important than these historical facts, the project of translation was initiated and completed in substantial faith and was bathed in many hours of God-fearing prayer. If the King James Bible does not represent the very Word of God, we have little hope of *ever* having it.

In her lengthy book *In Awe of Thy Word*, Gail Riplinger does an immense service for all those seeking reliable ancient Scripture in the 21st century.[64] Those who have rejected the King James Bible have abandoned a great treasure. When men like Brooke Foss Westcott and Fenton John Anthony Hort reject the Authorized Bible and look for an alternative to it in waste heaps, they are announcing to the

---

[a] Psalm 12:7

world that they doubt the ability of their Maker.⁶⁵ Almighty God *keeps* His Word just fine.ª

Anyone who belittles the final authority of Scripture honors himself above God. This condition defines much of mainstream religion around the world and especially in America. "Interpretation" has come to mean free-for-all. And yet, the Bible is *extraordinarily* clear on many things religious crowds consider debatable. Pride, apathy, laziness, and spiritual depravity are the real challenges—not interpretation. Sadly, a large number of churchgoers are putting themselves in the same category as blatant unbelievers. A lack of respect for the Scripture is a symptom of fetid pride. It betrays a fetish for *stolen* and manipulated truth.

Harris—a secular psychologist—suggests that human intellect can rightfully claim full credit for all moral truth. But he does not stop there. He believes that human intellect has the ability to write, as it were, a new book of moral standards—so that one day we will be able to consult with a moral expert and find truth.⁶⁶ (He seems to think that humans could improve upon the moral standards in Scripture.) In this way, the Author of truth is smothered out of mind, and at the same time, human achievement is copyrighted—like the many new versions of "scripture" on the market today.

The deceptive power of intellectual pride has disastrous potential. If we lean too heavily on our ability to reason, we will find ourselves in some slippery places. Harris—by his own admission—has had a significant role in damning thousands of souls. He writes, "As someone who has received many thousands of letters and emails from people who have ceased to believe in the God of Abraham, I know that

---

ª Psalms 12:6

pessimism about the power of reason is unwarranted."[67] The Book of Obadiah tells us that pride is deceptive.[a] People like the idea of being one up on God. It gives them a feeling of unrestricted superiority. We *ought* to have reason—the Bible commands it—but only if it is tempered by an appropriate meekness and gravity.[b] If we forget what side is up—our Maker's side—the reasoning power that we ought to run on takes a nasty spill, and we find our beloved vehicle tumbling through the scrapyard of oversold logic ... and ourselves, in turn, spiritually bankrupt.

Many believe in Darwinism because they think they are smarter than God. It is not about data. In a section headed "Trouble in the Creationist House" Pigliucci[p6] shamelessly confesses, "To refuse to accept that this particular debate [secular evolution vs. creation] is about ideology rather than science is foolish.... It is therefore urgent that ... [we] point out the internal inconsistencies in the creationist camp."[68] The Enemy has been driving wedges for centuries. He accentuates the pride and lust of wayward believers and pits brothers and sisters against one another. The central goal of all this work is to discredit God. And it is bound for disappointment.[c]

Reliable ancient Scripture teaches us the cure for this deadly pride. To the Nazi church Christ was a heroic warrior who hated the Jews, but this is not the portrait of Him the Gospels reveal. He loved His people and gave Himself for them with awesome humility. Geisler[p34] observes, "A sacrificial lamb—is the very antithesis of a man-made hero."[69] Most people over-advertise themselves, but this is not the

---

[a] Obadiah 1:3
[b] 1 Peter 3:15
[c] Isaiah 14:12-17

biblical way. The pages of Scripture instruct us how to think soundly. When we internally link the gifts of our Creator with our Creator, we will find our minds more *gifted*. When we practice sincere humility, we develop *solid* mental strength. But the humility must be sincere.

Sincerity is where most people run into problems. *Imitation* humility poisons every bit as much as *real* humility heals. The deeper people sink into pretenses the harder it is for them to come clean. If we stage humility, it tends to become a sitcom; eventually the prospect of sincerity becomes a joke.

Highly-educated scientists who have claimed—through their beliefs—that they are smarter than God have little room for true humility. Harris[p19] tries to bring humility into the picture. To defend his argument, he notes: "At any scientific meeting you will find presenter after presenter couching his or her remarks with caveats and apologies."[70] So long as people struggle to *inflate* their reputation, they must take great care to defend themselves from all the needles of criticism that could pop their ego balloon. The apologies presented at scientific meetings are planned beforehand as a means of *defense* rather than as an admission of fault. Defensiveness implies that someone thinks he is right. The kind of humility that prearranged, publicly-staged apologies most often display is *false* humility. Although there are a few stellar exceptions, scientists with above-average intelligence typically enjoy showcasing what they know, and often use well thought-out "apologies" to do so.

With that said, science really does by its nature require a constant stream of legitimate caveats and apologies. Solid confidence—such as the kind we need in order to build a sound life—is foreign to the scientific community. The bright-line statements of the Word of God provide bedrock that science *cannot*.

Confidence without pride is uniquely the product of biblical directives.[a] Unless we read the Book, we will tend to think too highly of ourselves. Arrogance flows naturally from ungodliness. But not even self-absorption can allow for the kind of confidence that reliable ancient Scripture affords. Self-inflated people will constantly run into nagging reminders of their many shortcomings. The struggle to find confidence apart from the Author of confidence makes for the most disappointing challenge of a lifetime. When Jesus preached, "people were astonished" because He taught with *true* "authority."[b] His authority was not a charade. He brought the Word of God to us—and that Word carries power.[c]

---

[a] Romans 12:1-3
[b] Matthew 7:28–29
[c] Hebrews 4:12

CHAPTER 2 REVIEW

STUDY NOTE: Modernistic philosophy is attacking and reversing the morality of the American people. This chapter explores the grim end and misleading nature of progressive rationale and reveals the diverse benefits and native honesty of traditional morals. The reader should note that the reliability of scientific discoveries is often contingent on the personal character of researchers and scientists. (See pages 198-202 for suggested answers).

THE TAPROOT OF IRRESPONSIBILITY:
1. Why is academic achievement without personal integrity dangerous?
2. What is implied by a person content with tolerance?
3. Why is tolerance alone weaker than real love?
4. Do some influential atheists believe moral absolutes are real?
5. What document signed 11-11-1647 initiated U.S. public education?
6. What was a stated objective of the U.S. public education system?
7. Why do many Jews prefer a political savior to a spiritual one?
8. What precise event fulfilled more than 300 Old Testament prophesies?
9. Did Darwin advocate or distain a mature sense of spiritual responsibility?
10. How would we expect Darwin's spiritual stance to affect his science?
11. What is a common response to matters of personal fault?
12. What drives some to willfully deny the Record Keeper's <u>existence</u>?
13. What does Dawkins say about Darwinism promoting atheism?
14. Is evil more elusive and dangerous when irresponsibility is allowed?
15. Harris says that what "serve as anchors to social and moral norms"?
16. If fear anchors moral norms, this implies what about "the rod"?
17. In what two ways will a parent who ignores his or her own faults fail at parenting?
18. Why do parents in the modern culture often murder their children?
19. In what way does Darwin's concept embody scientific welfare?
20. Compare Genesis 2:16 with 3:1. What key word is missing?
21. What are some dangers inherent in believing free will is an illusion?
22. What does the U.S. Supreme Court recognize as the basis of law?

THE TAPROOT OF NEGLIGENCE:
1. What is the spiritual and intellectual equivalent of financial depreciation?
2. What has allowed for widespread misunderstanding of the Bible?
3. What group restricted the circulation of Bibles during the Dark Ages?
4. What was the worst threat of illiteracy feared by American colonists?
5. In what way does factual content provide a basis for thinking skills?
6. In what Bible verse do we find "the circle of the earth"?
7. Who said, "The execution of the voyage ... is simply the fulfillment of what Isaiah had prophesied"?
8. What Bible verse tells us the Creator "set a tabernacle for the sun"?
9. In what way do many atheists believe that they are God?
10. How have proponents of Darwinism violated First Amendment rights?
11. What was the final ruling for the Scopes "monkey" trial of 1925?
12. What is one early symptom of a truth deficiency?
13. Is widespread violence and decay consistent with Bible teaching?
14. What is the true cause of such awful circumstances in this world?
15. How are strong moral laws similar to earth's gravity?
16. Who said, "It could be rational to strategically limit one's choices."
17. What is a good reason for having set-in-stone moral principles?
18. Do some secular scientists believe in a universal moral code?

THE TAPROOT OF DISRESPECT:
1. How does the form of the word "respect" break down?
2. Why do some of the optic nerves crisscross behind the nose?
3. If Earth's orbit could be illustrated by the circumference of a 2mm copper pellet, how big would our Milky Way Galaxy be in comparison?
4. Why does humanism tend to downgrade the natural world?
5. Have some secular scientists critiqued the order of the universe?
6. Dawkins said "The objects and phenomena that a physics book describes are simpler than" what?
7. How many events might be possible in a billion, billion years on earth?
8. What event assumed by most secular biologists would be categorically impossible given $10^{293,000,000}$ opportunities?
9. How do "heroes" influence psychological development?

10. What word often ascribed to God implies "wholeness"?
11. What provides a flawless, universal model for proper conduct?
12. How does Consequentialism suggest finding moral truth?
13. What is the harm in ceasing to think about "right" and "wrong" and pursuing instead what we think is the best route to human well-being?
14. How can negative consequences be a useful temporary means?
15. Why would Harris assume that the natural world must be "blinkered and susceptible...nearly ridiculous" if God is in control?
16. What reason does the Bible give for a predictable, orderly universe?
17. What reason do atheists have for a predictable, orderly universe?
18. In what direction does entropy cause evolution to trend toward?
19. Do evolutionists now think of evolution as progressive or neutral?
20. What does the use of neutral evolution as an explanation for the origin of biological structure imply about the quality of life forms?

THE TAPROOT OF SELFISHNESS:

1. What is selfishness?
2. Does selfishness seem to make good practical sense?
3. Why is selfishness an immature attitude?
4. What aspect of natural selection is highly emphasized by Darwinists?
5. After first life spontaneously happens, what is one of the first dead ends in hypothetical sequences for a Darwinistic history of life?
6. Who believes multicellular life forms were assembled by selfishness?
7. What human value strongly implies we are NOT merely selfish mass?
8. Who said "Love your enemies, bless them that curse you, do good to them that hate you, and pray for them which despitefully use you, and persecute you"?
9. The thought of genuine giving sparks a "warm glow" effect in the human mind. What is a good Bible explanation for this?
10. What is Jesus Christ warning against when He says, "If therefore the light that is in thee be darkness, how great is that darkness!"?
11. Harris finds, "Religious notions of morality ... are not exceptions to our common concern for well-being." Who in the Bible shows otherwise?

88 EXIT THE SPIRAL

12. Harris accuses religious people of being no exception to the rule of selfishness. How could a Christian be well challenged by his accusation?
13. Did New Testament writers generally have obvious earthly motives to promote or to deny the teachings of Jesus Christ?
14. Is selfishness a dangerous attitude in the development of morality?

THE TAPROOT OF PRIDE:
1. What major portion of Bible text was disregarded 11-13-1933 in Berlin?
2. How should most pride be defined?
3. There is a direct relationship between how much pride people allow and how far they drift from what?
4. Noah Webster traced the word "humble" to what old Latin word?
5. Who divided the human lifespan into eight developmental stages?
6. Why is resting in God's ability and finding Him capable the best way to advance through the eight stages that Erikson discovered?
7. What does Leviticus 26:19 imply about the nature of pride?
8. What did Adolf Hitler believe was the source of all earthly beauty?
9. How can a person maintain substantial beliefs?
10. Why do many scientists prefer the complex stories of Darwinism rather than accept the simple accounts of Scripture?
11. What does Dawkins refer to as "memes"?
12. What fun game illustrates the illogic of Dawkins' "memes" for truth?
13. Why is modern textual criticism often a horrible activity?
14. Why is the King James Bible superior to modern versions?
15. How do some Bible commentators seem to know that Mark 16:9–20 is "not part of Mark's original record"?
16. Is a lack of respect for the Scripture a common symptom of pride?
17. How has Sam Harris had a key role in damning thousands of souls?
18. What debate did Pigliucci say is "about ideology rather than science"?
19. What happens when we internally link the gifts of our Creator with our Creator?
20. What is a danger of staged humility?
21. How do the bright-line statements of the Word of God provide bedrock that science cannot?

CHAPTER 3
VITAL FAITH

—Faith is a widely misunderstood and essential element of conscious life. When the accuracy of certain information is confirmed in the heart of a person with total clarity, that information is recognized as truth. *Faith* is that deep and abiding sense of truth. To live and function intelligently, we all rely necessarily and largely on a faith of sorts; however, true and enduring faith is a divine awareness that is developed exclusively through God's Spirit and the study of God's Word. Common and scientific conclusions provide a degree of confidence, but such confidence is susceptible to changing, uncertain circumstances. Any genuinely reliable faith requires an accurate perception of *eternal truth*—it is the gift of God.

COGNITION

"Excuse me!" a voice calls. You turn to discover a strangely familiar face. But can it really be him? A classmate you haven't seen in 20 years stands before you. A name suddenly snaps to mind, and you eagerly start into a conversation. It's been a long time, but it seems like only days ago that you were sitting in that high school class together. What a rare treat to catch up on the events of the last decades.

Most of us can easily relate to this scenario, but we rarely evaluate such an event from a psychological point of view. The ability to recognize faces, even after many years without an actual encounter, is a common skill. But what are we remembering *technically?* Psychologists believe that our minds store pictures of the world around us. Those pictures—sometimes called phantasms—account for every detail of an individual's world. A majority of the faces and personal profiles that we mentally have on record we will never encounter again in this lifetime. Yet, we *know* that those files represent real persons or things.

Strangely enough, these phantasms are the closest that we will ever get to our physical environment. *All* the details of our world are stored as mental images. And, according to scientists, we *never* actually get to sense the immediate present. Greene[p9] discusses the point. "When I contemplate reality—what exists at *this* moment—I picture in my mind's eye a kind of snapshot, a mental freeze-frame image of the entire universe right *now.*"[1] Often we think of faith as it applies to the future, but science is finding that faith is every bit as necessary for the *present* as for the future.

So—we might ask—what is *the present?* It comes as a huge surprise to most of us that this simple question represents one of the deepest and most enduring questions of all time. Greene continues: "Anything you see right *now* has already happened." He says that our perception of now develops from "the things that we intuitively believe existed at that moment."[2] Since light takes time to travel, and we take time to process what we see, we always see what recently happened in the past. And so it is scientifically necessary that "we walk by faith, not by sight."[a] Our need for faith only deepens from here.

---

[a] 2 Corinthians 5:7

Not only are we incapable of *seeing* the present, physics has literally no *place* for the present. Greene recounts a conversation that German philosopher Rudolf Carnap had with Albert Einstein. "Einstein said that the problem of the now worried him seriously. He explained that the experience of the now means something special for man, something essentially different from the past and the future, but that this important difference does not and cannot occur within physics."[3]

Greene mentions the fact that "the laws of physics that have been articulated from Newton through Maxwell and Einstein, and up until today, show a *complete symmetry between past and future.*"[4] Our idea of now has literally no scientific basis. The whole concept of the present hangs entirely on a sort of *faith*.

We cannot even function without some kind of faith. Those who maintain that they have no need of faith are flatly out of touch with reality. As we discussed in the previous chapter, pride causes us to insist on impossible claims. We would all like to have perfect knowledge of our surroundings, but none of us comes close to having such knowledge. Faith is the only honest option.

Faith connects the dots. Even the fastest high-definition media displays use individual frames to create the illusion of movement. When we watch video output on a screen, we are connecting images. But connecting dots is not a trivial matter. Our universe embodies the ultimate illustration of faith.

All the particles of nature are connected. The term "universe" means "turned into one."[5] It is a testimony to the unified character of nature. There are no threads linking the particles of nature, but they are very literally tied together.

While this is not evident in our common experiences, at a super-microscopic level it *is* abundantly clear.

All the particles of nature are constructed of *energy*. Thus, as scientists seek to understand the fundamentals of nature, they are researching the basic unit of energy. A single unit of energy is called a quantum. Much has been invested to learn how these basic units of energy behave. We call this study quantum mechanics.

Quantum mechanics tells us that all the dots of the universe are connected. Greene reports: "Researchers confirmed that there *can* be an instantaneous bond between what happens at widely separated locations."[6] Although this statement references the findings of fairly recent experiments, the scientific community has known this for some time. Greene remarks, "The need to abandon locality is the most astonishing lesson arising from the work of Einstein, Podolsky, Rosen, Bohm, Bell, and Aspect."[7] In the study of quantum mechanics the idea of specific location often breaks down, and we find that the universe is *connected*. Two particles can behave in perfect parallel even when they are situated many miles apart.

Science is stumped. The scientific community marvels at the natural connection, but no one understands how it happens. Perhaps there is some unknown field that links all the particles of universe together, but the picture of faith that is on display here is awesome.

Reliable ancient Scripture tells us that nature is held together by God.[a] Whether it is a natural field or not, the power that holds nature together is ultimately the strength of

---

[a] Colossians 1:17

her Creator. And it works. The power that links nature together is very real. There is a common bond that links *everything*. This is a fact that science can observe, but not a fact that science can really explain.

We need faith to function mentally. Mental abilities are supported at every stage by a kind of faith. Psychologist Jean Piaget conducted extensive research on intelligent behaviors and found that the rational power of our minds is built one block at a time. As we gain information about a local environment, we develop little patterns of behavior that allow us to successfully interact with our surroundings. Piaget called these patterns "schemas." A schema is the basic building block for rational thought.[8] Over time we can adapt our schemas to conform to new information, but we cannot think rationally at all unless we have some schemas that we *trust*.

We need faith to *grow* mentally as well. Piaget found that there are four major stages of rational perception. When we feel that a broad category of our schemas is trustworthy, we can move on to another stage.[9] It follows logically then that without trust we become mentally handicapped—in the sense that we have no resources to move forward. Unless we draw some rather broad conclusions, we will be permanently stuck with a child's mentality.

Although Harris seems to understand this vital role of faith, he confuses the subject. He notes: "It is surprising that so little research has been done on belief, as few mental states exert so sweeping an influence over human life."[10] He also makes the important connection between faith and mental resources. He finds that "when we believe a proposition to be true, it is as though we have taken it in hand as part of our extended self."[11] But Harris is *not* consistent on this point. Earlier in this same book we saw how he asserted his personal opinion in which he *backhands* the idea of belief, saying, "Faith, if it is ever right about anything, is right by accident."[12] This is an important logical conflict that seems unreasonable to dismiss as a mere quirk. How does an intelligent man such as Harris misjudge the role of faith (belief)?

As we discussed in the previous chapter, pride misleads us with frightful stealth. We may not be able to function without faith, but that does not keep us from *claiming* that we are beyond it. Faith of any sort implies that *someone else* is trustworthy and that we can rest in *that* person's ability to stabilize our surroundings. Faith is not pride-pampering. It is necessary and honest. Proud people must overlook massive areas of their lives in order to feel in control of their world. That hunger for control blinds people to the beauty of truth and amputates their spiritual arms.

In the first part of chapter 1, we discussed the spiritual fall of the first generation (Adam and Eve). We are now in a better position to discuss the event. Functional relationships always require some type of faith; and faith, in turn, requires personal honesty. Honesty is twisted and lost through pride. If we think too much of ourselves, we will tend to think that we are independent—that we do not need help. As a result we will tend to get ourselves into a lot of trouble.

All the pain in our world traces back to a person who tried to claim spiritual self-rule.[a] He turned from the counsel of his Maker and decided that he would choose for himself what was right and what was wrong. And—as we are all finding out the hard way—he was much less qualified than he realized. With infinite wisdom the Creator stamped nature

---

[a] Romans 5:12

with obvious scars—road signs such as disease, parasites, predators, physical decay, and the like. They tell us that we need help. But these are *not* the greatest problems of our world.

In the purest, gentlest environment possible pride and its litter would corrupt families and destroy nations with even *greater* success. A child reared with all the conveniences of wealth will more often than not be spoiled. It is common practice, even, to assume that a spoiled child is from an affluent family. Conflict and pain mature us better than a silver spoon. The natural *pains* of our world give birth to spiritual sincerity better than any other physical influence. Secular arrogance not only started all the pain in our world but is also the primary *provider* of pain in our world. A tame environment is not the answer.

Faith is the answer. We need to believe the truth about ourselves and our nature. People are not as impressive as they let on. There is nothing dishonorable or unintelligent about recognizing our simplicity. On a personal level Albert Einstein was characterized most remarkably by his devotion to simplicity.[13] There is wisdom in simplicity! To deny our need of faith is arrogant and dishonest. Reliable ancient Scripture teaches us that true faith is a vital spiritual vehicle.[a] Godly faith allows us to seize the grace that our Maker offers us.

Saving faith is *not* a product of the human mind but rather a divine gift.[b] As the Holy Spirit of God works in our minds, He brings truth and humility that pride will not naturally admit. He stirs us in a way that our environment never could. He shakes us to the core, but He leaves *us* to

---

[a] Hebrews 11:6
[b] Ephesians 2:8–,9; Titus 3:5

make the decision. We are not guaranteed a second opportunity, yet most of us get several. Time after time the eternal King stops at the blind beggar's place, and often the King's invitation is declined. Hebrews 2:3 asks, "How shall we escape, if we neglect so great salvation." The universe offers no greater opportunity. The life of Jesus Christ and His Blood were given for *us*. What a waste is pride!

We possess a remarkable capacity for spiritual life. John 3:8 illustrates spiritual responsiveness by comparing spiritual stimuli to physical wind: "The wind bloweth ... so is every one that is born of the Spirit." The leadership of the Spirit in a person's life presents a phenomenal mystery. When we are in sync with the Spirit of God, we will respond to His slightest intimation. In this way we become the Body of Christ. As a healthy human body simply responds to its own natural mind, so the Body of Christ is capable of responding to the Spirit of Christ. Individuals who walk with Christ become part of God's literal body. First Corinthians 12:27 tells us, "Now ye are the body of Christ, and members in particular." The link between Christ the Head and us—the body—is faith.[a] Faith puts our Head on right.

---

[a] Romans 12:1–5; Ephesians 4:13

VISION

With all the force of 10 quadrillion (that is 10,000 trillion) freight train engines our planet shoves away from the nearest star. Like the body of a child clinging with white-knuckled fingers to the outer bars of a spinning merry-go-round, under the force of such tremendous weight our world seems ready to tumble off into space at any moment. Unlike the wide-eyed child, though, our planet has no arms to secure it. Yet, the earth cannot break free. For many centuries we have glided around the sun in a smoothly rounded orbit—secured by nothing but the invisible arms of the sun's gravity.

Like gravity, faith is a real property of a nearby object. Hebrews 11:1 defines faith as "the substance of things hoped for," which tells us that true faith has actual *substance* to it. Thus, when the Holy Spirit reports historical or future events to us, we are experiencing biblical faith. As discussed at the end of chapter one, we know scientifically that the past and future are physically etched into nature. However, as a general rule, we are blind to most of the events of the past and all the events of the future. Biblical faith *reveals* details about those physical events to which we would otherwise be oblivious. Faith is spiritual vision.

What we sense as gravity is really a ripple or warp in the fabric of space and time. We are literally slipping into an indentation made by another object. When we get close enough to a large thing, we begin sliding down the slope of its spacetime dimple. That tug that we feel *evidences* a nearby mass. In the same way, the unyielding faith of believers convicts and informs the lost souls around it. Hebrews 11:1 also explains to us that faith is "the evidence of things not seen." Faith not only provides sharp vision for those who *experience* it, but it also brings light to those who *witness* faith's effect on others. Godly faith *itself* is evidence of timeless truth. Biblical faith provides spiritual sight for believers and a lamp of guidance for the lost.

We need faith to see. Whether or not a person believes the truth of Scripture, beliefs are essential to personal development. None of us can do without beliefs. A businessman who has no belief in his business is destined for bankruptcy. A scientist who has no belief in her work can plan on making little progress in her field. And a dad who has no belief in his children will tend to father unmotivated couch potatoes. At every level belief provides us with vision, and vision drives us from day to day. But unlike natural beliefs, biblically-based faith *never* ends in disappointment. By living in biblical faith we get to experience some beautiful events that are far beyond our circle of natural influence. Godly faith equips us with high-resolution spiritual eyesight that produces accurate images of future events.

The development of every functional system requires vision. Mechanical engineers, architects, and designers in general must have strongly creative minds. We have little respect for a designer who throws his products together recklessly. We expect a person whose livelihood is design to think through all the details before fabricating a thing. Good design requires much *insight*. When we get a glimpse of what will happen in the future, we can effectively plan for it. This is how functional systems are born. Insight powers invention.

Evolution has *no* exemption for this rule. As we saw in chapter 1, real evolution accounts for nothing but "change."[14] Evolution has no rational means for creativity. It remains poetically ironic that Darwinists chronically miss the bottom line here. Life patently testifies to an immensely creative power. Its message resonates with unmistakable clarity. Yet, only a minority of scientists seem to rise to the natural reveille. Many secular scientists appear to be, in a sense, sleepwalking through our world. Logic-based evolution functions to explain how the sophisticated systems of our world *express* the information that was creatively designed inside of them. Real evolution says *nil* about the origin of useful complexity—and it certainly *does* nothing to design it.

Darwinism is a dreadful daydream that attests to the dangerous potential of immoderate human imagination. It is a comedic drama that uses science as its clown. The greatest achievement of Darwinism is widespread disrespect for the complexity of the natural world. Many public schoolchildren are taught that life sprang into existence by accident and then continued to develop and bring us up to the present through a long series of additional accidents.

According to secular biologist Ernst Mayr, "What Darwin called natural selection is actually a process of *elimination* [emphasis added]."[15] Evolutionists know this. Darwinists assume that everything happened by accident, but they beat around the bush like madmen. If natural selection bubbles down to "survival of the fittest," where did the fittest come from? Natural selection has no eyes to see the real world and no mind to shape it.

Computer scientists have built a program that supposedly simulates the reproduction of natural organisms. Once it is initially activated the program is designed to automatically and endlessly reproduce itself. As this program begins to multiply itself, it will occasionally make errors—the rough equivalent to biological mutations. Not surprisingly, the project really did produce some randomly adapted programs. Science writer Carl Zimmer declares triumphantly, "What the successful digital organisms shared in common was a short program. In each case, mutations had stripped them down to the simplest program that could still replicate."[16]

By adding unnecessary information to working programs, the scientists hoped to demonstrate the usefulness of these random errors. The researchers found that after thousands of generations, simpler programs began to emerge and that these became the most abundant versions. As it turns out, faults in the replication of the program really did, in a way, purge some of the end products. The shorter programs reproduced more quickly and eventually became more numerous. But it seems as though the experiment revealed the nature of natural selection *too* well. If the concept of natural selection were capable of influencing real life forms, it would tend to *reduce* complexity—the opposite of what Darwinists believe (that simple life forms evolved into more complex ones).

Natural selection tries to explain how nature could kill all the lame individuals of a population. There is no provision for *positive* development in the concept of natural selection. This fact is painfully and irrefutably logical. Darwinists understand this but then turn around and make unfounded claims as if they did *not* understand. Mayr later writes, "We believe that ... traits were *acquired* [emphasis added] by natural selection or, if they arose by chance, their maintenance was favored by selection."[17] Selection means *removing* less fit mistakes—it has no power to *invent!* The power to invent *cannot* be a logical result of natural selection. How is there any confusion at this point? But it gets worse.

Some Darwinists simply run with this precedent of denial. Highly acclaimed secular biologist Richard Dawkins,[p5] for instance, just builds on the idea of creative natural selection as if he could *reinvent* the rules of logic. He imagines that in "the case of living machinery, the 'designer' is unconscious natural selection, the blind watchmaker."[18] That is like the old tale of walking to and from school all uphill *both* ways. Natural selection has no creative abilities. Denying this fact is just plain illogical.

Real adaptation is not what the Darwinists usually emphasize and is not at all what Darwin had in mind. Darwin pictured adaptation as an open-ended process of development. In his travels he came across certain species that had significant degrees of variation. Darwin was entirely ignorant of the relevant genetic mechanisms that caused the variation that he observed, and he assumed that there were no restrictions on it. Given what we now know about genetic science, that is *not* the case.

As Darwin plotted his defense of accidental origins, the real explanation of evolution was being developed by a most unlikely individual. An Austrian *monk* growing peas on the property of a monastery discovered that pea variations occurred in predictable patterns.[19] The patterns he documented carried much greater scientific import than Darwin's footloose concepts. That monk, Gregor Mendel, had revealed a genetic cycle.

Mendel found that some genetic traits are *hidden*. A vast collection of features is available in the genes of a living thing. But many of those genetic blueprints stay concealed through dozens of generations. What Darwin saw as novel variations were actually ancient traits that had remained out of sight for some generations. The information had been there the whole time. Like godly faith that genetic information had long represented what would one day be flesh. In other words, faith provides inside information about unseen physical events, similar to the way recessive traits represent hidden information that will at times be expressed physically. Thus, Darwin had found nothing new.

A Punnett square is a simple tool that shows how a variety of hidden traits work statistically. Living things that have two parents usually have *two* genes for each genetic location. If one gene is considered "recessive" it will hide its trait from any other gene that shares the location. On the other hand, if a gene is "dominant," it will tend to dominate its partner. Some genes have more complex relationships, but for genes that are truly dominant or recessive, only one gene type actually produces a trait. If the gene for green-colored pea pods is recessive, a plant specimen that grows green pea pods suggests that *both* of its pod-color genes are recessive. In the Punnett square below, the little box with two lower-case *y*'s represents a small group whose pods look green. All other plants, including the parents, would have pods with a different color.

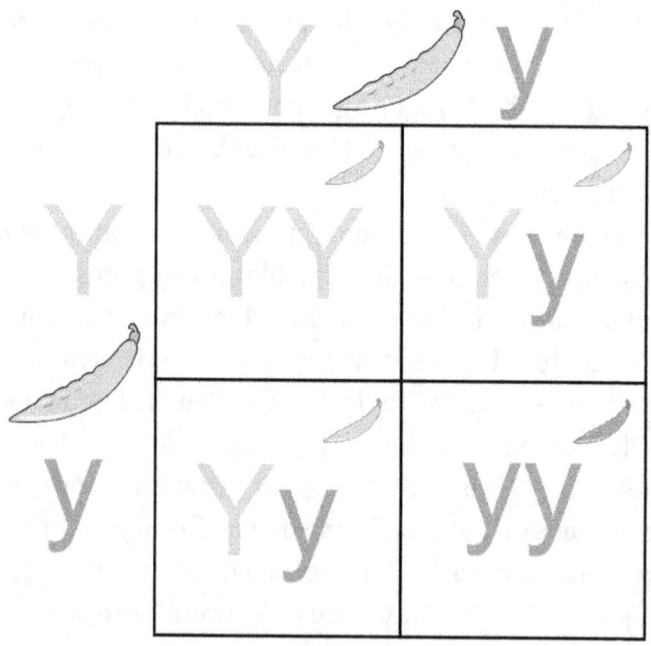

Although this is basic high school biology in our day, it seems Darwinists still have not grasped the deeper import of it. All the variation necessary for observed adaptations is accounted for perfectly by ancient genetic information. We are *not* finding anything new. Mayr understands that the "process of adaptation is a strictly passive one."[20] In other words, adaptation does not go about making new traits. Rather, it uses what already *exists*. Mayr defines adaptation more clearly. "The legitimate use of the word adaptation is for a property of an organism, whether a structure, a physiological trait, a behavior, or anything else that the organism *possesses* [emphasis added], that is favored by selection over alternate traits."[21] Darwinists know that science tells us this, but they reject the greater implications.

If all the information necessary for useful adaptations has existed for an indefinite period of time, then evolution, which says nil about where that information came from, explains nothing of truly original significance. All we need to understand variation has been long written in the genes. And there we find great potential.

Reliable ancient Scripture teaches us that the Word of our Creator is alive.[a] God invented creativity and He is the Master of it. His vision knows no boundaries. Although genes are very particular, they allow for an awesome spectrum of possibilities. Consider the range of human genetic traits.

We know that no two people are exactly the same, but how does that work on a genetic level? Our Maker has installed thousands of traits in the human genome. If we view these traits individually and simply assume that a given trait is either "on" or "off," we can calculate the number of possible

---

[a] Hebrews 4:12

combinations. For example, if there were only five possible features to look at, we would calculate two combinations for the first feature, then multiply that answer by two for the second, and so on. That means that there are 2×2×2×2×2 or 2^5 combinations for an individual with five features of this kind. Thirty-two combinations may not seem especially impressive, but when the working space is extended to *thousands* of traits, we calculate an astronomical number of possible combinations.

Let's pretend there were only 300 human genetic features. That would calculate out to a minimum of 2^{300} possible combinations. That is a very big number. The United Nations has estimated that as of 2017 there were about 7.5 billion people on earth. If the world population were 10 million *times* the 2017 estimate and the average lifespan dropped to only 50 years, the population could continue for 10^{75} years without two identical individuals. That means that such a human population could live the entire length of secular evolution's speculative timeline (15 billion years) more than 10^{64} times with *only* unique individuals. That is 100 trillion times for each atom of the earth. And we are just getting started on the *real* number of combinations. The number of combinations possible for the *thousands* of real traits is not even within the range of meaningful illustrations. That testifies to some *serious* creativity built into our genes.

Darwin was entirely ignorant of this genetic potential. Like most of the scientific community of his time, Darwin knew nothing of genetic patterns. The average 19th-century scientist viewed reproduction as an orderly process designed by the Master. They had respect for the process of reproduction and recognized it as a divine fingerprint. But they had oversimplified the truth. As a result Darwin was reared in a scientific community that passionately rejected any major variations of species. Scientists typically thought that significant differences between generations would suggest the presence of ungodly chaos. Because he was ignorant of Mendel's research, Darwin brashly assumed that large-scale variations among species represented a glitch in the orderliness of nature. He thought that the changes were spontaneous—that nature was demonstrably unordered.

Darwin felt that natural trends of variation were quirks that discredited the authority of Scripture. He suspected that variation was open-ended and that nature could do as it pleased—that there were no boundaries. Darwin once wrote that the idea of species variation was "like confessing a murder." Some have commented regarding this statement that the murder was the murder of *God*.[22] Darwin's supporters should not, however, rally around his affirmed ignorance of genetics. Trends of species variation may have been obscure in Darwin's time, but the science behind those trends speaks in strong *support* of the written Word. Our respect for God should be *amplified* by the awe-inspiring display of creativity found in the genetic potential before us. Without a reasonable degree of *faith*, however, we will miss the message every time. Darwin's disciples are apt to grope like blind folks even in the brightest sunlight of natural revelation. They often have a pitifully undernourished faith, a deficiency that leaves them suffering with a severely blurred vision.

Innate genetic potential has been drawn out and *observed* on a very broad scale. Dawkins reveals the fact that "selective breeders experience difficulty *after* a number of generations of successful selective breeding. This is because after some generations of selective breeding the available genetic variation runs out."[23] Dawkins suggests that this beneficial genetic variation can eventually be replenished by mutation, but that is simply guesswork. What we *know* is that breeders can draw out amazing traits with available genetic variation.

Faith allows us to see beyond our circumstances, and the science of genes provides an excellent illustration of this relationship. So much of the wealth that genes have to offer hides out of everyone's view. There is more potential in a person's genes than any of us could discover in an eternity. What we *see* is so small a part of God's work in our lives. James 4:14 explains that a lifetime passes like a vapor. We are all tiny pilgrims passing over massive fibers of the Artist's eternal canvas.

The monarch butterfly is quite a pilgrim as well. The Author of creativity has designed the genes of these tiny insects with amazing instincts. Consider the extraordinary life cycle of a fourth-generation monarch....

Somewhere on the underside of a milkweed leaf a monarch butterfly lays her egg. After about four days, a tiny worm emerges and begins devouring the poisonous milkweed leaves. Inside the little larva are special tissues that allow it to absorb the poisons safely. After a time of feasting, the caterpillar attaches itself to a surface and tears its skin off to reveal a beautiful creamy green interior. For several days the little chrysalis dangles like a gold-studded emerald right where the larva attached it. Then—slowly—the color begins to change. The outer skin of the chrysalis begins to clear, revealing a vibrant orange color. Gently, after 10 days of hidden change, a butterfly emerges. The wings gradually unfold to reveal a tiny masterpiece. Although she looks nearly identical to her mother, she is built for a much different life.

As the fourth generation of the year, this tiny insect has great ambitions. Today she begins a trek that her parents, grandparents, and great grandparents never knew. Fluttering her way across huge expanses of North America, she steadily makes her way to a certain oyamel forest in Mexico. There, after carrying her featherweight body *3,000* miles, she takes a greatly anticipated three-month winter rest as did her great, great grandparents. As February draws to a close, she leaves the forest and starts back.[24] But she will never make it. She has lived *seven times* as long as her parents,[25] but the flight home will take generations of *others,* her descendants, who fly by their Maker's wisdom.

Just as instincts guide the behavior of animals, so we can be guided through the *written* Counsel of our Maker. We need the wisdom of Scripture more than we know. Without the Roadmap of Scripture we will wander aimlessly like nomads in a dry wasteland.[a] The Sword of the Spirit—like a surgeon's scalpel—can analytically divide the landscape of our life with skillful precision; and yet the same Book can bind together the loose strands of our life as nothing else can.[b] Without the Word, we discover that we have no real reference point—we are hopelessly lost. Aside from the written Truth, there is no point on which to spiritually navigate—no True North to help us find our way, no stable reference point to gauge progress, and life must necessarily be pointless in general.

Without the Anchor of Scripture, our life is adrift on a billowing sea and ultimately seems worthless. During the past 10 years, some 36,900 or more Americans have taken their own lives each year—with the number per capita *increasing* almost every year.[26] They have acted literally on a godless worldview.

---

[a] Psalm 119:105
[b] Ephesians 6:17; Hebrews 4:12

When ego-centered people realize that the universe does not conform to their *personal* judgments, they are traumatized; they are humiliated—their *god* dies. Life without God is life wasted, and it crushes the human spirit. Those who worship only themselves or human intellect are generally classified as "atheists," but true atheists—those who are strictly *without a god*—are logically prone to suicide.[a] In a strict sense of the term, an atheist is a person who sees no central purpose for living.[b]

Without Gospel Truth even those who are successful by social standards lose interest in life. Proverbs 29:18 teaches us that "Where there is no vision, the people perish." We need an objective for our lives. Anything short of the true Word of God will always leave us wanting. As Proverbs 29:18 continues, it gives a healing insight: "but he that keepeth the law, happy is he." Keeping the law means that we protect it as a cherished possession. As we do so, the Truth of Scripture brings joy into our lives as no human philosophy ever could.

Sam Harris[p19] testifies to a stark personal experience that he had with an acquaintance of his:

> I once knew a very smart and talented man who sent an email to dozens of friends and acquaintances declaring his intention to kill himself.... I sent several emails urging him to seek professional counseling, to try antidepressants, to address his sleep issues, and to do a variety of other obvious things to combat depression. In each of his replies, however, he insisted that he was not depressed. He believed himself to be acting on a philosophical insight: everyone dies eventually; life, therefore, is

---

[a] Ephesians 2:12; 2 Thessalonians 2:4
[b] Exodus 15:2; 2 Samuel 22:33; Colossians 3:4

ultimately pointless; thus, there is no reason to keep on living if one doesn't want to.

We went back and forth.... These communications seemed to nudge him away from the precipice for a while. Four years later, however, he committed suicide.[27]

Without reference to the Truth, how could anyone refute the man's logic? It made perfect sense in his meaningless worldview. Truth is what gives us purpose that never fades. As we progress through the stages of our life, we all face many disappointments. Some of us have found a Lighthouse to guide us through those dark waters of life, while others are lost at sea. The light of Truth makes all the difference. The word "lodestar" was originally used to mean the North Star, but over time it has come to mean "chief inspiration." The background of this word illustrates our discussion well. As a general rule, the light that truth brings guides us *and* motivates us in a vital way.[a]

Scripture causes us to focus on a much larger sphere, and its influence challenges us to live beyond our natural shortcomings. Compassion for others flows from the image of God stamped on the human soul.[b] Yet, we grow selfish easily. Psychologist Paul Slovic has found that when we are confronted with the needs of one person we tend to be more compassionate than when we are confronted with two cases. The larger the needy group is, the less prone we are to care about the situation.[28] It is sad, but it follows naturally that our limited resources limit our compassion.

---

[a] Psalm 119:105, 130
[b] 1 John 4:7

Although the well-being of world populations is a burden too great for any of us *naturally,* God cares, and He gives us the right heart when we spend time in the Word. Matthew 14:14 shows the Source of our compassion. "Jesus went forth, and saw a great multitude, and was moved with compassion toward them, and he healed their sick." Awesome ... where human compassion comes to an end, the Lord's compassion is just warming up.

The steady stream of men and women giving their lives as missionaries ranks as one of the supreme displays of divine compassion in the lives of ordinary people. The deep compassion that these saints express for whole nations shines brightly as the work of godly faith. How can they see the needs when so many others have turned a blind eye? Faith is the answer. Godly faith focuses our spiritual senses and allows us to catch sight of things much bigger than we are—much bigger than our lifetimes.

The recent surge of media has served to confuse its consumers more than perhaps any other influence in recorded history. If a picture speaks a thousand words, then we are getting information overload. Between television and the Internet, we are force fed much more than we can chew. The net result is spiritual murk. The faith that flows from reliable Scripture allows us to see large significant aspects of our world and beyond, but the innumerable particles of disconnected information pouring from diverse media sources serve as spiritual static.

Our vision has been overburdened and our spiritual eyelids are growing heavy. Americans are drinking lies like water and have misplaced the Truth. We need to find faith within the Holy Word of God again.[a] In the sacred pages of reliable Scripture we learn of faith—we see the world in focus.

---

[a] Psalm 94:9

EDUCABILITY

Based on Fred Gibson's novel published the previous year, the 1957 film *Old Yeller* endeared a big yellow dog to much of the American public. In the movie, Yeller came to a 19th-century Texas family as a stray and won the heart of a young boy named Arliss. As the plot progresses, the dog eventually proves to be a valuable friend to Arliss' skeptical older brother, Travis, as well. But, Old Yeller doesn't make it to the end of the story. While defending the family from a rabid wolf, Yeller takes a bite and is fatally infected with rabies. In just a few days, the family's loyal friend turns into a rabid monster—attempting, at one point, to *maul* Arliss. Everything the family dog once loved has become untrustworthy in his mind. He is even terrified of water. The rabies virus has destroyed Yeller's brain. Finally, in a hugely famous scene, Travis shoots and kills Old Yeller.

Hardened unbelief dries human minds like spiritual rabies. Learning is fueled by faith; without faith a person mentally dehydrates. One of the most distinctive symptoms of the rabies virus is fear of water. In many cases fluids cause the voice box of an individual with rabies to spasm wildly.[29] This is why rabies was once commonly known as hydrophobia— fear of water. When people lose faith, they stop drinking the truth that surrounds them. A surface of unbelief will always repel the water of truth. Knowledge can take root and grow only in the absorbent soil of belief. All attempts at education are futile in the absence of faith.

If we lose faith in our God-given potential, our personal growth dries and shrivels. Although the film *Old Yeller* is an exceptionally mild motion picture (especially by the horrific standards of our day), even at this tame level, a variety of industry-standard hazards accompany it. Watching the film, people are *entertained* by the pain of others. The more people view the pain of others as a source of entertainment, the less they feel a burden to help. Over time they detach themselves from the real needs around them. They begin thinking of themselves as passive viewers rather than active influences. The scene in which Travis fires his rifle and kills Old Yeller sends emotional shock waves through viewers, who are shaken emotionally to see such things.

When viewing a fictional video, however, viewers are shaken for no good reason. A stream of false alarms will tend to dull people to real, dead-serious events. As a result, they grow emotionally unstable or calloused.[a]

After years of treating feelings like playthings, it should come as no surprise that life in general seems uninteresting. The typical American views over *two and a half hours* of television per day![30] And they are not watching much *Old Yeller*. The ungodly undertone of motion pictures in the 1950s has grown into a putrid cesspool of bald-faced filth.[b] The public drinking water offered by most 21st-century media is disgustingly corrupt, and quality control has become a sloppy sham—asleep at the faucet. The net result is spiritual confusion of pandemic proportions. When the imagination is being used more as a toy than as a tool, people have a hard time believing anything. A passion for *life* is growing fearfully scarce. To recognize the God-given value of human life and the world around us requires belief—faith. And only a sense of *value* can adequately prompt the work of learning.

---

[a] Lamentations 3:51
[b] Psalm 101:3

Although dangerous influences are more accessible than wholesome ones, we all need to trust someone in order to learn. Though we might not like to admit it, we cannot learn without trusting others. In a search for answers we are bound to trust the word of another person at some point, even if we try to research a subject ourselves. Pigliucci[p6] admits: "Using somebody's advice limits our choices and biases them in certain directions. But we have no acceptable alternative."[31] Rather than wading aimlessly into a sea of raw information, it is most advisable to consult an expert. By nearly anyone's standard this is practical wisdom. The question is not whether or not we *ought* to place our trust in others (we must trust someone), but *whom* will we trust? It is often very difficult to determine who is trustworthy.

Reliable ancient Scripture teaches us that the "heart is deceitful above all things."[a] That means that we would do well to double-check our *own* motives and conclusions.[b] Harris[p19] discusses some research on the matter. Even he believes. "The general finding of this research is now uncontroversial: we are poorly placed to accurately recall the past, to perceive the present, or to anticipate the future with respect to our own happiness."[32] We need help. But the help that we need is not going to be found by a secular scientist—as Harris would argue—but rather in the precious pages of Scripture.

The Word of God is a Treasure Chest of wisdom that we can bank on. As the Author of rationality, our Maker is entirely equipped to provide perfectly reasoned counsel for our lives. Trusting His Word is one of the greatest

---

[a] Jeremiah 17:9
[b] Proverbs 11:14; 24:6

opportunities afforded to us in this lifetime.[a] We know that a spiritually lost person cannot understand the value of superhuman wisdom, and unfortunately Harris illustrates the point. He grumbles indignantly, "Skepticism about the power of reason leads, more often than not, directly to the feet of Jesus Christ."[33] He must mean trying to reason away the sins that we know we have. That reason ... because it failed. But there was never a real question. Perhaps we *are* a little skeptical of our own reasoning when we see it in the light of perfect Truth. It only makes sense. Once we get a taste of that heavenly wisdom nothing else compares.

The Apostle Paul compares the Old Testament Law to the Gospel of Jesus Christ. The Gospel is so awesome that it outshines even the immense beauty of its Old Testament foundation. Paul concludes: "Seeing then that we have such hope, we use great plainness of speech."[b] When God gets a hold of us and we get a glimpse of what He has done for us, there is little room for flowery speeches. His essence is just plain humbling.

We learn in faith what we could not learn without it in a million lifetimes. While we each have only one lifetime here, we also have millions of testimonies of those who have gone before us.[c] If we do not value the principles the previous generations of saints have learned and passed down to us, we will waste the fruit of countless lifetimes. As mainstream religion pushes to keep pace with cultural trends, the church

---

[a] Proverbs 3:5-6
[b] 2 Corinthians 3:12
[c] Romans 15:4

is losing touch with her heritage.³⁴ We would do well to study the lives and works of earlier saints.[a] The lessons are endless.

Faith is the solid material on which all spiritual understanding is constructed. Without deeply planted footers to build upon, all the lessons of a lifetime can begin to shift and splinter—eventually leaving people spiritually ruined. Proverbs 23:10 warns, "Remove not the old landmark." Without points of reference people will overstep their bounds and get disoriented in a foreign landscape.

When we wrestle against unfamiliar powers, our only hope is to find our base and keep it strong. A wrestler who is careless about his footing will find himself in a suffocating pin in short order. We must keep our base strong, or we will never have an opportunity to learn anything but the discomfort of defeat.

All that we need to learn is right before us. Species variation illustrates this point well. To those who are unfamiliar with the laws of genetics, the wide diversity of species within a closely related group seems like evolutionary magic at work. But when we learn the principles of genetics, we find that none of Darwin's mythology is necessary. All the useful combinations ever expressed have been available since creation because in the real world nature has no power to invent healthy genes.

As a general rule, genes stay the same; but the products they produce range widely. The modern synthesis of evolution clearly states that "hereditary variations are based on particles—*genes*—that *retain their identity as they pass through the generations; they do not blend* with other

---

[a] Jeremiah 6:16-17

genes."[35] Of course, the evolutionary synthesis also immediately proposes that all the existing genetic options were conceived by random mutation—a scenario that is mathematically impossible. One fact is clear: Geneticists know—from observation—that the immense variation typical of natural populations is the direct result of impressively stable, *existing* genetic information. And while evolutionists routinely classify unfamiliar variations as novel mutations, they have known for decades that useful variations are properly classified as ancient genetic possibilities.

All that we can learn in a lifetime has been learned before; we can only discover uncommon ways of looking at the same old facts. Genes don't even look at the facts subjectively; they don't think for themselves. Genes do not comment on the information they have. They parrot it. Genes are loyal secretaries—*not* executive officers. Genes transcribe the Master's program; they have no power to devise it. He programmed the genes to be used in different combinations but as specific information. Evolution shuffles what has been provided. Mayr[p8] explains: "Recombination in a population is the major source of the phenotypic variation available for effective natural selection."[36] Phenotypic variation means variation in the actual bodies. The diverse physical traits that we observe in the natural world are the product of shuffling the same old genes.[a]

The possibilities are practically endless. Although genes work within clearly defined parameters, the number of combinations that are possible within those limits approaches infinity. In math the set of natural prime numbers (2, 3, 5, 7,

---

[a] Ecclesiastes 1:9-10

11, 13, 17...) is infinite even though it excludes most numbers.[37] Defined systems are not necessarily small systems. When we calculate the number of genetic possibilities for a human, we would like to imagine that any physical feature can be described in one of two ways. But in the real world features have more than two options. Often genes work together. Dawkins[p10] observes: "Large numbers of genes whose effects add up are called polygenes. Most measures of ourselves, for instance our height and weight, are affected by large numbers of polygenes."[38] This concept radically increases our understanding of the total innate capacity of our genetic variation tank. How do we begin to calculate such a wealth of designed potential?

A very small fraction of the information available in our genes ever gets used. Even as an individual develops physically, most of the cells conceal their information. The blueprint for our eyes can be found in our toes, but it is not expressed there. In a living body each cell contains its own copy of the whole body's genetic instruction manual. The instructions are acted out only when appropriate. Dawkins recognizes that "in any one place in the developing body, at any one time during development, only a minority of the genes will be switched on."[39] The information exists but will educate the proteins only at the relevant moment.

True faith allows us to learn and provides us with information that science cannot. This is not to say that science does not work, but rather that science is *impotent* apart from some degree of faith. All learning must be based on a foundation of faith. Teenagers who think they know everything know little and learn less. It is a great day when we learn to listen to those who have wisdom—to those who have walked the path ahead. Godly faith provides a drink of cool water in a rabid and ungodly culture.

CHAPTER 3 REVIEW

STUDY NOTE: This chapter defines several forms of faith. Secular proponents often assume that there is a sort of dichotomy between them and the "believers." They propose that they live by fact whereas religious people live by faith. In this chapter we see that faith is, in some respect, a way of life for literally every person on earth. We also see how Bible-based faith is distinct and why it is so important for spiritual health. (See pages 202-205 for suggested answers).

THE FAITH FOR COGNITION:
1. What is a name for mental images that are used for memory?
2. Why do we never experience the immediate present?
3. Why did Einstein say "the problem of the now" deeply worried him?
4. How does faith "connect the dots" of life?
5. What is the essential meaning of the term universe?
6. What do the particles of nature all consist of in a general sense?
7. What is a single unit of energy called?
8. How can two particles be in perfect natural parallel while miles apart?
9. What did Jean Piaget see as a basic building block for rational thought?
10. Piaget felt that a person can move into a new major stage when?
11. In what way is a person who lacks trust mentally handicapped?
12. Faith of any sort implies that who is trustworthy?
13. How does a hunger for control blind people to the beauty of truth and amputate their spiritual arms?
14. In what way do disease, parasites, predators, physical decay, and the like provide spiritual "road signs"?
15. Why do we need the Holy Spirit to provide spiritually saving faith?

THE FAITH FOR VISION:
1. In what way is true faith like gravitational force?
2. How is true faith like spiritual vision?
3. How does faith bring "light" to those who witness faith's effect on others?
4. Can a "non-religious" person make progress without beliefs?
5. What type of mind do mechanical engineers tend to have?
6. "What Darwin called natural selection is actually a process of..."?
7. In the "survival of the fittest" where did the fittest come from?
8. Would natural selection logically reduce or increase complexity?
9. What contemporary of Charles Darwin discovered genetic cycles?
10. How are recessive genetic traits a good illustration of godly faith?
11. What simple tool is used to show how genetic traits run statistically?
12. If the only gene for green-colored pea pods is recessive, what would we assume about a plant specimen that actually grows green pea pods?
13. Why is the process of adaptation strictly passive?
14. How many combinations come from 7 features each going 1 of 2 ways?
15. What did Darwin assume about large-scale variations in a species?
16. Why was the idea of species variation "like confessing a murder"?
17. Why would selective breeders have trouble after many successes?
18. Monarch butterflies that migrate south may live how many times the full age of their parents?
19. What happens when ego-centered people realize that the universe does not conform to their personal judgments?
20. How are those who worship only themselves or human intellect generally classified?
21. Why are those who sincerely have no god prone to suicide?
22. How does the etymology of the word "lodestar" illustrate the motivating influence of truth on our lives?
23. How do some Christian missionaries have genuine enduring compassion for whole nations?
24. How do graphic media outlets often impair spiritual vision?

CHAPTER 3 REVIEW

THE FAITH FOR EDUCABILITY:

1. What is one of the most distinctive symptoms of the rabies virus?
2. Why are attempts at education always futile in the absence of faith?
3. What is a danger in being entertained by the hardships of others?
4. How much television does a typical American view per day?
5. What is a mortal danger of using imagination more as a toy than as a tool?
6. What personal trait allows one person to receive facts from another?
7. What does the Bible teach is "deceitful above all things"?
8. Why would Harris write that having faith in the teachings of Jesus Christ conflicts with sound reasoning?
9. What have geneticists identified as the basis of biological variation?
10. According to Mayr what is "the major source of the phenotypic variation available for effective natural selection"?
11. What set of natural numbers is infinite yet excludes most numbers?
12. What are polygenes?
13. Why are most of the genes in a developing body never activated?
14. How do genes illustrate the educating power of true faith?

CHAPTER 4
POTENT APPEARANCE

—Though appearances are very shallow indeed, they often form the basis of scientific discovery. Because science is bound inextricably in this vulnerable relationship (that is, it relies heavily on observation), it is critical that we establish a sound concept of appearances. Although it is quite logical to conclude that things *are* in fact as they appear, as a matter of practicality, we should exercise care to avoid deceptive images. More often than not, unfortunately, images are used as a manipulation tool. Media can leverage images with surprising and hellish success—and does so on a daily basis. Given the unusually influential nature of appearances, the topic warrants an aggressive study.

WEIGHT

Plunk. Only a short distance from the place of his birth 23 years earlier, he watched an apple fall. Isaac Newton began to build upon this rather mundane event.[1] He had felt the weight of that little fruit as it loosed from its branch and plummeted to the surface of the ground beneath. As an attentive young man, he saw the true weight of that falling apple and shook the scientific community with it.

Although we must learn to see beyond appearances, appearance often carries with it a relevant degree of meaning. Not only are theoretical models of nature most convincingly *confirmed* by observation, but quite often they are also *discovered* by observation. Most of the great scientific achievements throughout history have been the fruit of a few observant individuals. If we fail to draw inferences from what we see, nature will remain forever obscure. Science in general will never advance beyond what can be seen. And thus it is quite fair to conclude that natural science must always dangle on a string of appearances—many instances of which are surprisingly common.

When observations converge on common themes, we can often state *laws* that define the tendencies of natural events. Unless a given scenario is repeated several times, there is no hope of validating a natural law. Symmetric appearances feed the scientific community. If two independent laboratories record the same findings for a given study, it is most reasonable to believe that a lesson can be learned from the data. Greene[p9] notes that scientists often tend to trust theories that "*feel* right." He explains that "ideas of symmetry are essential to this feeling."[2] In other words, natural symmetry forms the groundwork of scientific laws.

It is interesting to note that symmetry is one of the most common evidences of intelligence. While it is easy to focus on the practical aspects of natural symmetry (scientifically calculable events), a deeper question is lingering here. Why is the universe consistent anyway? Greene observes: "The symmetries of nature are not merely consequences of nature's laws. From our modern perspective, symmetries are the foundation from which laws spring."[3] Universal symmetry is a natural cause *not* a natural result. The consistencies that science is built upon have no scientific explanation. The universe appears to display an immensely intelligent design.[a] It is a well thought-out and integrated system. The symmetry living things display so abundantly also provides a powerful testimony of intelligent artistry. Those who see life as a recycle bin of reused genetic garbage have no room to talk about biological symmetry. In his book *The Blind Watchmaker*, Dawkins skips the topic entirely. He discusses a computer program he built to simulate the creative potential of errors. The program draws two-dimensional figures that can be randomly mutated. To make the figures look roughly like living things in the real world, though, Dawkins *programmed* his computer to always keep figures symmetrical.[4] He proceeds awkwardly into his case with an astounding disregard for symmetry. This is a poor approach and leaves much to be desired logically.

While the discussion of symmetry seems elementary enough, it remains a worthy but rarely addressed consideration in the field of biology. Many animals—including vertebrates—have two *symmetric* eyes. We also know that humans, as well as many animals, use their eyes *together* for depth perception. If the eye were actually the chance product of gradually accumulating genetic errors, we would not expect it to have an identical partner on the opposite side of our face. Although it is certainly helpful and logical to have two eyes (and precisely what one would expect of an intelligent design), Darwinism must always rely on genetic mistakes that somehow just happen to work.

Although secular evolutionists routinely overlook this fact, the concept of natural selection possesses no minute trace of insight. As far as secular scientists are concerned, natural

---

[a] Hebrews 13:8; Malachi 3:6

selection is strictly dependent on lucky genetic errors. Scientists who believe a human eye is just a selected pile of fortunate mistakes must swallow that belief with a generous helping of fanciful imagination. Darwin said, "To suppose that the eye ... could have been formed by natural selection, seems, I freely confess, absurd in the highest possible degree."[5] In Darwin's mind, the development of an eye was only remotely imaginable if it occurred in gradual intermediate stages, with each stage serving a definite purpose. To make matters worse for him, the degree of purpose Darwin thought reasonable is now universally rejected as hopeful but unrealistic theory. And while it is very bad math to imagine that the massive complexity of an eye could develop through natural errors, the innate testimony of biological *symmetry* puts us center field in a whole different ball game.

As the Internet grows in popularity, there are more and more applications of secure sites. The convenience of paying bills, ordering merchandise, and transacting a variety of personal services is available thanks to a clever device known as the password. In order to set up a password, most sites will prompt us to *reenter* our password information. It is generally safe to assume that if the eight password characters in the first field match the eight in the second, the password characters were typed purposefully. This is a small-scale picture of what is displayed by biological symmetry—but not with merely eight matching characters but with *millions*. The Master entered thousands of matching password characters over and over and over again. Every time we see biological symmetry, a lengthy password has been entered twice. This sends an unmistakable message—what you see is no mistake!

An interesting note here is that symmetry is *not* typically essential to survival. Our kidneys, which are every bit as complex as our eyes, are usually impressively symmetric; but they do not *need* to be so. My mother was born with only one functional kidney, and yet she gave birth to *10* well-nourished children on it. To date, she remains in good health.

Whether or not we can see His work, our Maker does not make mistakes. Every time natural science works, it heralds a message of God's consistency. The only reason that we have a physically stable world—that we can interact with our world in a sane manner—is owing to the constancy of Almighty God. Denying this fact is possible only if we bury our heads deep into the sand of humanistic philosophy. The whole natural world trumpets the point of the Creator's constancy.

If all of nature appears to highlight the accuracy of reliable ancient Scripture, who are we to claim that it does not? Atheistic scientists must work rather hard to ignore the most obvious implications of nature. In his book *What Mad Pursuit*, Nobel laureate Francis Crick writes, "Biologists must constantly keep in mind that what they see was not designed, but rather evolved."[6] Dembski[p24] comments on this point: "If a creature looks like a dog, smells like a dog, barks like a dog, feels like a dog and pants like a dog, the burden of evidence lies with the person who insists the creature isn't a dog."[7] Everything about nature tells us that it is designed.[a] There is an instinctive awareness built into every man, woman, and child.

Living things are not only fantastically complex but also aptly suited. Mayr[p13] recognizes an "astonishing perfection" in the specialized abilities of existing life forms. He observes that each structure and behavior of every living thing

---

[a] Psalm 19:1–4

seems to be surprisingly appropriate.[8] The natural world does not at all appear to depend on a series of errors. It looks very much as if it were wisely conceived.

Natural laws do not result in the net progress of specified complexity. Natural laws break things down; they do not construct purposeful systems. The second law of thermodynamics states that natural systems tend to evolve toward *disorder*. Although the second law is a very general principle, it carries immense weight in the natural world. According to physicists the natural *decay* of the universe is what defines our moments—the second law literally sets the pace of time.

Greene comments: "The second law of thermodynamics seems to have given us an arrow of time."[9] This casts Darwin's concept of natural progression in a new light. If time is equivalent to natural decay, expanding the timeframe of nature only serves to *amplify* the degree of natural disorder. As Darwinists continue hot gluing eons onto their timeline, they are—at the same time—burning their concept to the ground.

The universe appears to have been designed. An invisible power saturates all of nature. Physicists have recognized that such power exists, but struggle to explain it. Many believe that there is an unseen field at play. They have labeled it the "Higgs field." Yet—to date—there is much mystery about it. Writing in 2004, Greene hoped that the European Center for Nuclear Research (CERN) would soon discover particular evidence of the Higgs field. And such evidence was, in fact, found by researchers there July 4, 2012. Regarding the Higgs field Greene made this intriguing remark:

Without invoking the spiritual, therefore, we may well closely brush up against the thinking of Henry More ... in our scientific quest to understand space and time. To More, the usual concept of empty space was meaningless because space is always filled with divine spirit. To us, the usual concept of empty space may be similarly elusive, since the empty space we're privy to may always be filled with an ocean of Higgs field.[10]

The Higgs field stands no doubt as a result and as a witness of our Savior's power. Colossians 1:17 reminds us that "by him all things consist." And we do not need astrophysics to know this.

One of the most fascinating truths about our awareness of God's existence is the phenomenal ease with which we recognize His presence. *Children* sense God. Harris reports: "Several experiments suggest that children are predisposed to assume both design and intention behind natural events—leaving many psychologists and anthropologists to believe that children, left entirely to their own devices, would invent some conception of God."[11] Contrary to Dawkins' "meme" concept, no one needs to train a child to believe that there is a God. We know it intuitively. Although this instinct in no way takes away from the fact that we need to study the Scripture to understand who God is, it is still an amazing truth.

Nature reveals more of her mysteries than we realize; her Author has built her that way. If we fail to recognize the lessons on nature's surface, we can hardly hope to grasp her deeper mysteries. While science is incapable of answering our deepest questions, studying what is clearly visible allows us to tap into the available resources that science offers as effectively as possible. To overlook what is immediately before us is both boorish and wasteful.

PLASTICITY

While Isaac Newton was drawing truth from the things he saw, a young rebel was learning the art of manipulating veneers. William Chaloner became a highly successful 17th-century con artist who produced a huge wealth of counterfeit coins and notes. He talked his way out of jail on several occasions by artfully shifting blame and often slid stealthily under the noses of officials unchecked. At one point he even attempted to gain a leadership position in the English Royal Mint. While Chaloner was spending time at Parliament, Newton—Master of the Royal Mint—happened to recognize him from an earlier encounter. A few years later, it was Newton who gathered several witnesses against Chaloner and finally put an end to the deception of this masterful manipulator. The brilliant Chaloner met his fate on the gallows of Tyburn, on March 16, 1699—his name no more than an ugly scar on the pages of history.

Appearance is a potent influence in our lives, but it tends to be dangerously *plastic*. Over the years professional manipulators such as Chaloner have grown in popularity. Many of them have impressive credentials and respected titles, but they are still—more than anything else—experts at fabricating mock surfaces.

Likewise, Darwinism draws much of its strength from professionally doctored images. We are shown a series of figures that begin with a hunched little ape and end with an erect modern man, and the subtle details of the illustration artfully stir our thoughts. Pictures can sell us on fictional concepts more effectively than we might expect. Scripture warns us that the eye affects the heart.[a]

The 19th-century embryologist Ernst Haeckel was sharply aware of the impact that skilled drawings can have on us. He was responsible for a series of embryo sketches that seriously impacted Darwin.[12] Haeckel believed that the early stages of an individual's physical development provide an insight into progressive evolution of the past. He drew several images depicting the developing embryos of a wide range of vertebrates, and they all looked similar! Because it was somewhat difficult for scientists to get a firsthand look at embryos of a given age, the scientific community widely accepted Haeckel's work. Many scientists began to claim that the development of an individual body recaps the evolutionary stages of its species. They couched this fanciful notion in a technical-sounding catch phrase "ontogeny recapitulates phylogeny." Trouble was, it was all a sham.

Haeckel had drawn the figures deceptively. Devout secular evolutionist Stephen Jay Gould openly admits that the forgery was the "academic equivalent of murder."[13] But to this day those same images are being circulated in American high school textbooks. The lies continue, though we have known for many decades that real vertebrate embryos do not look like Haeckel's creation and that similarities between actual embryos relay no relevant evolutionary meaning whatsoever. For over a century Haeckel's artwork has corrupted scientific thought and has borne testimony to the deadly power of warped pictures.

Although Haeckel's case of mass deception is unusually obvious, it is not unusual. Darwinists have a bad habit of

---

[a] Lamentations 3:51

linking grossly unrelated species together and then drawing pictures to smooth out what doesn't work. As the Chief Science Writer for *Nature*, Henry Gee expertly confirms, "To take a line of fossils and claim that they represent a lineage is not a scientific hypothesis that can be tested, but an assertion that carries the same validity of a bedtime story—amusing, perhaps even instructive, but not scientific."[14] Darwinists invest too much in artwork and not enough in science.

With even a basic understanding of genetic variation, we find that the grand proposals of many Darwinists look pitifully inadequate. With any knowledge of genetics, we should expect diversity. And among a diverse population it is very common that similar individuals are attracted to similar niches. Races and subspecies develop as a result. Mayr clarifies that "this process of the multiplication of species is something entirely different from the phyletic evolution of species in a fossil lineage."[15] In other words, the diversity *within* basic types is not to be confused with the *origin* of types.

The Lake Victoria cichlids that we discussed at the beginning of chapter 1 serve as a strong illustration of this idea. Mayr acknowledges that "different feeding types of cichlid fishes can still originate, but all are still cichlid fishes."[16] Of course they are. An alert high school biology student should be able to come to that same conclusion.

Yet, somehow a large number of secular evolutionists seem to miss the link between predictable genetic cycles and the fossil record. We should not be looking for Darwin's theoretical intermediates (or missing links) anymore—we know that genes work within a restricted window of variation. We haven't found the intermediate links because they do not make sense genetically and thus could have never existed literally. All that we will ever find in the fossil record are members of distinct species groups.

A wealth of unfamiliar species has been fossilized in the strata, but not a single meaningful intermediate. The emphasis that Darwinists place on extinct species is almost comical. Mayr declares, "The most convincing evidence for the occurrence of evolution is the discovery of extinct organisms in older geological strata." Lest we think that these extinct organisms show some sort of progression, Mayr explains this "evidence" in his next paragraph. "New types often appear quite suddenly, and their intermediate ancestors are absent in the earlier geological strata."[17] If unrelated extinct species are the most convincing evidence of large-scale evolution, we should wonder what could be less convincing.

But it gets worse. Mayr asserts: "No well-informed person any longer questions the descent of man from primates and more specifically from apes."[18] He feels that "the evidence for this conclusion is simply too overwhelming."[19] What exactly does he mean by evidence? He suggests three areas of *similarity* between apes and people.

First, the living species of apes look roughly humanlike. Apes have all the comparable organs and structures that a Darwinist would be looking for. This may seem significant to a Darwinist, but it certainly does not confirm their philosophy. In reality, the similarities between man and ape do not provide any evidence of a physical relationship—it is only implied by secular ideas. *Grasshoppers* have hundreds of structures that are roughly paralleled in humans, but these structures do not prove a common descent any more than they prove a common Designer. Apes are much more similar to humans than grasshoppers, but the point here is that similarity is not to be confused with proof of common descent. Darwinists have been trying to redefine the meaning of biological similarity ever since their philosophy was conceived. The biblical worldview has always been a much more realistic explanation of comparative anatomy, especially when considering the vast similarities of genetically disassociated life forms.

Second, the extinct species of ape look roughly humanlike. This should not be a surprise since, as a general rule, extant apes look similar to people today. Sadly, Darwinists have a habit of announcing "new-found missing links." They are all meaningless. Whether the "links" are legitimate fossils or deliberately manipulated hoaxes, the substance of every "man-ape link" is either human or ape—and perhaps an occasional pig's tooth. Surely there are extinct ape species that look different from living apes, but none of these realistically suggests a link between ape and human. That suggestion is no more than an interesting speculation.

Third, there is a significant degree of similarity between human genetic material and that of the chimpanzees. We share certain genetic sequences with chimps; but with over 100 million genetic differences, it is not nearly as many as Darwinists let on. Human genes cannot all even be compared one-on-one with those of chimps—at many points chimpanzees have a different genetic addressing system.[20]

If we are overwhelmed by such evidence, it is to our shame. In a section titled "What Is The Actual Fossil Evidence?" Mayr explains the details behind what evolutionists call hominids—a meaningless title given to any extinct ape that they consider a potential link to humans. Mayr reveals emphatically: "Virtually all of them are somewhat controversial!"[21] He is still mincing words a bit. The fact of the matter is that *no one* has *anything* that distinctly fits as a man-ape link. As a logical study of genetics would predict, there is zero evidence to support all the clever images that Darwinists have created for us.

Physical similarities usually present more of a *problem* to Darwinism than anything else. The eye of an octopus, for example, is very much like a human eye, yet other points of common resemblance are shockingly sparse. We could find some corresponding sequences of DNA that we share with octopuses as well, but would a rational person claim that they imply common ancestry? Even the most fancifully minded evolutionist would struggle to imagine the descent of a human from an octopus.

Identical organs and genetic sequences appear in a huge assortment of remarkably dissimilar species—clearly indicating a common Designer. When these similar or identical structures appear in starkly dissimilar species, Darwinists must assume that the parts developed independently and just happen to look alike. Dawkins[p10] discusses the issue:

> New World army ants resemble Old World driver ants. Uncanny resemblances have evolved between the quite unrelated electric fish of Africa and South America; and between true wolves and the marsupial 'wolf' *Thylacinus* of Tasmania. In all these cases I simply asserted without justification that these resemblances were convergent: that they had evolved independently in unrelated animals.[22]

This is difficult for evolutionists to conceive.

In their attempt to avoid such instances, Darwinists use a principle known as "maximum parsimony."[23] The principle maintains that scenarios involving *less unrelated similarities* are more believable. All the disconnected parallels do not look good for Darwinists. As a rule, they do their dead-level best to avoid their Maker's fingerprints. It is not easy, and it is definitely not scientific.

As we saw in chapter 1, Darwin's tree of life has no place in the real world. But that has not stopped the attempts of modern Darwinists. To avoid the frustration of real-world data, many secular evolutionists have fabricated scenarios of natural history using pure imagination. Dawkins reveals that they use only "the relatively few trees that do not too drastically violate their preconceptions."[24] (So much for the scientific method of basing theories on observable data and minimizing the role of presuppositions.) Others have abandoned the concept of logical descent altogether. Zimmer[p14] imagines, "Our common ancestor was every microbe that lived on the early earth: a fluid matrix of genes that covered the planet."[25] Darwinism is literally quack science.

The patchwork is endless. Similarities are a problem for Darwinism, but so are differences. Two species may share a variety of large physical features and still look enormously estranged on a molecular level. Instead of accepting the natural implication that the species are not physically related, Darwinists just paste new sections to their timeline. Although it is bad biology, many evolutionists believe that with enough time molecules can work out their differences. Mayr finds that a "reconstruction of the date of origin of an animal phyla with the help of a molecular clock methodology reveals a far earlier origin than indicated by the fossil record."[26] The molecular clock is a time scale based on microscopic differences produced by the DNA of various plants and animals. So Darwinists simply award broader differences a longer time to even out. Darwinists have made a kind of science for redefining the clear molecular contradictions to their concept. True scientific evolution describes only genetic cycles. From a purely rational point of view we should not expect major species groups to link together. Genetic principles bar the possibility. Darwinism turns out to be merely a weak speculative branch of good evolutionary theory. Darwin believed quite a bit of science fiction, and his disciples are still pursuing some of his fanciful concepts. *Mendel* did a much better job of explaining how evolution works. There is nothing revolutionary about real evolution—*it does not affect origins*. It is a series of predictable cycles, and there is *nothing* progressive about it. Real-world evolution shows us how 500 varieties of cichlid can develop from a few individuals. It shows us how hundreds of dog breeds can result from a single pair. It's all about expressing the volumes of information that the Author of life has given us. Real-world evolution honors the Master; it does not belittle Him.

Surprisingly, modern definitions of evolution actually tend to *verify* its practical significance, even though Darwinistic philosophy is always skulking in the shadows nearby. Pigliucci[p6] uses a common description of evolution— "a change in the frequencies of the genes found in natural populations."[27] This explanation is perfectly accurate. There is no logical conflict until Darwinistic philosophy is superimposed upon the definition. In other words, variation within preexisting groups is the full extent of real evolution.

Many people mistake Darwinism for good (i.e., real) evolution, and a few even confuse it with biology in general. Harris[p19] has a hard time with those of us who aren't hoodwinked by his beloved philosophies. He complains, "Despite 150 years of working at it, we still can't convince a majority of Americans that [secular] evolution is a fact. Does this mean biology isn't a proper science?"[28] No. It means that the illogical versions of evolution are not proper biology. The issue is a single overemphasized topic within *one* of the fields of biology. We would do well to recognize it as such.

Many scientists have also been sloppy in their identification of genetic traits. Evolutionists are often guilty of calling an unusual trait a mutation when in fact no mutation took place. Futuyma[p18] notes, "In practice, many mutations are still [2009] discovered, characterized, and named by their phenotypic effects. Thus we will frequently use the term 'mutation' to refer to an alteration of a gene from one form, or allele, to another, the alleles being distinguished by phenotypic effects."[29] In other words, mutations are not typically confirmed on a genetic level; rather, they are *assumed* based on examination of larger physical characteristics that the organism in question expresses. So, as hidden genetic traits are revealed, evolutionists regularly accuse the unfamiliar traits of being genetic mistakes. In this way mutations are often suggested without cause.

As we saw in chapter 3, genes have significantly more potential than the average person realizes. When scientists lean on mutations it reveals their ignorance of genetics. Skin color and other race-associated characteristics are examples of innate genetic capacity. Although races of human look drastically different, the genes that make the difference can be hidden for many generations. Human genes are nearly identical throughout the world. This came as a great surprise to early geneticists. Zimmer notes: "Many biologists once thought that races carried dramatically distinct sets of genes. Some even went so far as to claim that they were separate species. But research on human genetics now shows that these

POTENT APPEARANCE: PLASTICITY 139

old ideas were wrong."[30] We can learn volumes of information from existing genes. Genetic errors are *not* instructive.

Modern Darwinism thrives on the journalist's sleight of hand. Trivial genetic cycles can be proclaimed as huge paradigms of evolutionary progress. Futuyma presents a classic instance—bacterial resistance to antibiotics. "The same bacteria are back, but now they are resistant to penicillin, ampicillin, erythromycin, vancomycin, fluoroquinolones—all the weapons that were supposed to have vanquished them."[31] Evolutionists do not typically emphasize this fact, but there were bacteria that were resistant to a variety of antibiotics even before the first antibiotics were in use. Antibiotics have not caused any new bacterium to develop; they have simply caused an increase in the percentage of bacteria that are resistant to the antibiotics. As it turns out, antibiotics tend only to draw out previously *hidden*, uncommon traits. And, in reality, what Futuyma envisions as "an explosion of evolutionary change"[32] is—in his own words—simply the "same bacteria" but in new ratios.

Four-winged fruit flies provide another hobby horse. Darwinists cite the development of these mutant flies as a shining example of positive mutations. The facts about these tiny insects, however, do not support such statements. Fruit flies have two normal wings for flying and two little wing-like structures for balancing themselves. The two little wing-like structures, known as halters, are formed through a complex developmental process that actually restrains one set of normal wing genes. Because of genetic restraint on the second set of potential wings, a normal fruit fly is aerodynamically efficient, having one set of flying wings and one set of halters to balance itself out. By breeding three mutated fruit flies, scientists were able to develop a fruit fly with four full-size wings. Essentially the mutations that were used each had a part in blocking the complex genetic sequence that restrains the development of the halters. In other words, four-winged fruit flies had not actually gained wings; in a genetic sense, they had simply lost critical restraints. The information (or genetic blueprint) on how to produce a duplicated pair of wings had been built into the healthy fruit fly and was present all along.

Not surprising is the fact that the second set of wings is limp and serves as a major handicap to the hapless mutant.[33] In his very revealing book *Icons of Evolution*, Jonathan Wells puts it this way: "What the four-winged fruit fly shows us is that mutations can shut down a complex network.... Damaging a complex regulatory network with mutations doesn't explain how the network originated."[34] Genetic accidents are *not* helpful.

Conceptual plastic surgery is common practice in the Darwinist camp. They routinely dismiss the second law of thermodynamics using a shallow, imitation of logic. Pigliucci argues: "The fact that living organisms are ordered systems does not necessarily mean that they violate the second principle. If that were the case ... *we* [emphasis added] could not build roads or houses, or for that matter even keep our bedrooms clean."[35]

The orderliness common to all life is definitely *not* a contradiction to the second principle, but it absolutely *does* beg for an initial organizing agent. All the best examples of organizational progress involve either intelligent forces or pre-existing biological structures. The Darwinist *assumes* that this biological structure is the product of *un*intelligent forces. And as a result, Pigliucci would see the development of an egg as a prime example of nature's organizing itself. Although he understands that the egg is simply running its pre-established program, Pigliucci believes that nature built the program in the first place. But the problem remains—where does nature demonstrate self-organization in any degree remotely similar to biological structure? The use of existing life to explain the origin of life is not acceptable (and is similar to the logical fallacy known as circular reasoning).

Shape-shifting is not unique to Darwinistic biology. Psychologists can play the same game. Harris tells a story about parents who starved an 18-month-old child because the child wouldn't say "amen" before meals. According to Harris, what we can learn from this incident is that the parents "suffer from religion."[36] While most Christians are appalled by this account, Harris apparently thinks it represents a typical Christian home. Later he alleges that he does *not* use the "most extreme forms [of religion] to represent the whole." He says that he merely takes "the specific claims of religion seriously."[37] The world knows no love greater than Christian love,[a] yet the ungodly have warped appearances so radically that many can see only those cases in which Christianity has been corrupted. There is certainly no Scriptural basis for the parenting practice of starving a child!

Using a house of twisted mirrors, Harris and others have worked to strip the modern world of hope. He has practically convinced himself—and godless masses—that we are all animated dirt balls. In his troubled mind, we are each a literal pile of organic tissues and *nothing* more. He denies not only the existence of human free will but contends passionately that none of us has a soul.[b] He feels that "the idea

---

[a] 1 John 3:17; 4:21
[b] Genesis 2:7

that there might be an immortal soul capable of reasoning, feeling love, remembering life events, etc., all the while being metaphysically independent of the brain, seems untenable given that damage to the relevant neural circuits obliterates these capacities in a living person."[38] Damage to the brain *should* limit the soul's overall influence, in the same way that a flat tire limits a motorist's influence—the mind is the vehicle of the soul. Flats do not, however, amount to a reduction of the driver's presence. They affect the car—not the driver per se. In many ordinary ways we expect personal influence to fluctuate throughout a *person's* life. Why shouldn't our relationship with our brain follow the same rule? Harris understands many principles of the human mind but lives ignorant of his own soul. Without spiritual honesty—without Holy Spirit conviction—Harris will never truly understand who and what he is.

If we ever hope to learn beyond appearances, we will need first to see the *true* substance of what is already before us. Surfaces tend to be plastic, but the truth beneath them is not. Pay attention. Jesus said, "Who hath ears to hear, let him hear."[a] Repeatedly the words of the Savior echoed parables—everyday events that teach eternal truth. Right beneath our noses, in front of our eyes ... He has scattered life lessons for us to grasp spiritually. Appearances can forge our thoughts. But beware. Artificially forged surfaces have become big business.

---

[a] Matthew 13:9

CHAPTER 4 REVIEW

STUDY NOTE: In this chapter we assess the inherent meaning and influence of appearances. True science will always be built upon many careful observations; and observations, in turn, are always based upon appearances. We are naturally apt to believe what we see, yet images tend to be very plastic; and tend to be, as a result, a popular instrument of deception. With the increase of technology modern societies have been flooded with images (many deceptive), so that the relevance of this topic is escalating by the day. (See pages 205-207 for suggested answers)

THE WEIGHT OF APPEARANCES:
1. How are theoretical models of nature to be discovered and confirmed?
2. How does natural symmetry form the basis of scientific laws?
3. What is one of the most common evidences of intelligence?
4. Charles Darwin said, "To suppose that the eye ... could have been formed by natural selection, seems, I freely confess [what?]."
5. What secret personal code allows us to make purchases online?
6. Is symmetry required for survival?
7. What is the reason that we have a physically stable world and can interact with our world in a sane manner?
8. Nobel laureate Francis Crick said that biologists have to constantly keep in mind that the things they see are not actually what?
9. What law of thermodynamics sets the pace and direction of time?
10. What would an expanded timeframe for natural history allow?
11. What field includes an invisible power saturating all of nature?
12. Why was the concept of empty space meaningless to Henry More?
13. Where does the Bible say "by him [Christ] all things consist"?
14. What are children predisposed to assume about nature and origins?

THE PLASTICITY OF APPEARANCES:
1. Who was a very successful con artist exposed by Isaac Newton?
2. What did Ernst Haeckel believe about developing embryos?
3. What technical sounding phrase means that the development of an individual embryo, shows the Darwinistic descent of its whole species?
4. Stephen Jay Gould said that Haeckel's drawings are equivalent to what?
5. Who said "To take a line of fossils and claim that they represent a lineage is not a scientific hypothesis that can be tested, but an assertion that carries the same validity of a bedtime story— amusing, perhaps even instructive, but not scientific"?
6. How can races and subspecies develop with death as no factor?
7. What do Lake Victoria's 500 species of cichlid still share in common?
8. Why should we no longer be looking for Darwin's theoretical intermediates (missing links) in the fossil record?
9. Why is the emphasis that Darwinists place on unfamiliar fossilized species practically comical?
10. Are body structure similarities evidence of common descent?
11. Why should it not come as a surprise that the body structure of extinct ape species is somewhat similar to the body structure of humans?
12. How do genes show that apes are not literally related to humans?
13. What are hominids?
14. What is maximum parsimony?
15. Why would molecular clock methodology predict a very early origin?
16. What is a weak speculative branch of good evolutionary theory?
17. What is an accurate definition of evolution given by Pigliucci?
18. How do many biologists mistakenly assume that mutations have suddenly occurred?
19. Why did some biologists once believe that there were several different species of human?
20. How are the same bacteria back and now resistant to antibiotics?
21. How did a loss of genetic information result in a four-winged fruit fly?
22. All the best examples of organizational progress involve what?
23. How can a soul be independent of the brain, if brain damage can obliterate the mental abilities often attributed to the souls influence?
24. What are parables?

CHAPTER 5
THE SETTING

—Here we are for now, living out our years on this little planet in the Milky Way. Life is amazing! So many concepts (many held to be "facts") have come and gone, but reality just plods on with its own definite, unrelenting, simple *facts*. Living in this vast universe is such an astounding experience that it does sometimes seem surreal. The reality of nature, however, has quite sobering and precise implications that greatly limit possibilities—regardless of how soundly reasoned those possibilities may seem. The orderly universe we live in is a matter of fact and embodies both accuracy and wonder. Natural science must conform to this setting as a prerequisite for validation.

JURISDICTION

He was not exactly a professional golfer, but to him the world looked rather different on that day. Over the course of just a few minutes, he had set two all-time golf records. On February 6, 1971, Alan Shepard was the first person to drive a golf ball from the surface of the moon. His spacesuit was a little stiff; so he had to swing with just one arm. But on his second attempt, it seems he one-armed a golf ball over *300 yards*. Not bad for an amateur.

Context drastically influences the set of natural possibilities relating to a given event. Driving a golf ball 1,000 yards on level ground with conventional golfing equipment may be no big deal in the moon's low-gravity, low-friction environment; but it is absolutely impossible for a normal person to do so on the *earth*. A setting creates definite natural boundaries—a physical jurisdiction. The Author of natural laws is not at all restricted by them, but natural *science* is. Natural science must work within the framework of physical laws. Any scientific conclusion that involves an actual location must submit to the local conditions. In some cases local provisions form a *key* factor in the development of reasonable theories. Not all reasonable concepts are realistic. In fact, there are far *more* attractive ideas being circulated in our culture than there are accurate ideas. The difference is that inaccurate ideas will dissolve logically when immersed in real circumstances.

For 490 years the church has been resonating with a song Protestant reformer Martin Luther penned.[1] In English the first sentence proclaims, "A mighty fortress is our God, a bulwark never failing; our helper He, amid the flood of mortal ills prevailing." Like Abraham 35 centuries before him, Luther found that our Creator is dependable through all the trials of life—that He will not and *cannot* fail.[a]

Our Maker is perfectly competent in every situation, and His promises remain *always* true.[b] From the darkest corner to the brightest realm, His counsel is *impeccable*. The prophesy of Isaiah—penned 27 centuries ago—stands firm in the face of all the doubt and hate leveled against it: "No weapon that is formed against thee shall prosper; and every tongue that shall rise against thee in judgment thou shalt

---

[a] Deuteronomy 31:6
[b] Psalm 119:160; 2 Corinthians 1:20; Hebrews 10:23

condemn. This is the heritage of the servants of the LORD, and their righteousness is of me, saith the LORD."[a] Those who respect the guidance of the only wise God become part of an unshakably good heritage. Through godly respect we will become involved in something much greater than ourselves.

Those without God will always find their way either to principles that are consistent with reliable ancient Scripture or to disappointment. The natural environment itself allows for no other option. All the fantastic concepts of secular reasoning have at their center a dark and hollow pit. Harris notes: "It is now an article of almost unquestioned certainty, both inside and outside scientific circles, that science has nothing to say about what constitutes a good life."[2] He disagrees with this common sentiment.

Harris believes that science *does* have answers for our deeper questions. He believes that the good life is all about genes and external factors, and he provides us a picture of it. "Due to a combination of good genes and optimal circumstances, you and your closest friends and family will live very long, healthy lives, untouched by crime, sudden bereavements, and other misfortunes."[3] That all sounds wonderful; but the real world is not built like that, and neither are *we*. When we have it all by the world's standards, there will always be a nagging, hollow pit inside. (Probably similar to the one inside Harris' friend who opted to commit suicide even though, admittedly, he was not depressed.) Satisfaction is a gift of *God*.[b] We need Him.

Despite all the intellectual gifts he has been given, Harris refuses to receive the import of his own research.

---

[a] Isaiah 54:17
[b] Ecclesiastes 3:13; 5:19

Harris observes: "Population ethics is a notorious engine of paradox, and no one, to my knowledge, has come up with a way of assessing collective well-being that conserves all of our intuitions."[4] The pursuit of durable morality without reliable Scripture is bound for failure.

A natural context will often purge misconceptions—especially if we pay attention. Natural laws are beautifully consistent. They provide valuable benchmarks from which we can learn. Even amid the phenomena found at a subatomic level, there is order. Zimmer[p14] discusses this impressive regularity. "You can't predict exactly when a particular atom will decay, but a large collection of them will obey certain statistical laws.... The laws that govern atoms don't submit to any simple intuitive sense, but they work."[5] We can set our watches by the decay of radioactive particles; the environment is that methodical.

Carbon 14—often called radiocarbon—is a radioactive carbon that is an excellent example of this natural consistency. So long as it is not interrupted, it will take 5,730 years for half the carbon 14 that's buried around the world to become a stable form of nitrogen. That length of time, 5,730 years, is known as the half-life of C14. No one seems to know why it is so routine, but scientists and historians will stake a lot on it. Not only is C14 dependable, but particles of it can be found almost anywhere on the earth's surface. These two characteristics make C14 exceptionally useful.

In earth's current environment there is about one atom of C14 for every 1 trillion stable carbon atoms. Anything that eats, breathes, drinks, or draws from its surroundings in any way likely ingests C14. Because of this, every person, plant, and animal alive today contains an average of about one part C14 to 1 trillion parts stable carbon. And so, if any one of us were to die and be buried today, 5,730 years from now a carbon test would show about one *half* part C14 to 1 trillion parts stable carbon—assuming of course nothing had interrupted our remains. After 11,460 years there would be about one-*fourth* part C14 to 1 trillion parts stable carbon. This is a well-established scientific principle. Science cannot explain why C14 has such a reliable half-life, but we *do* know that it is *very* consistent.

The regularity of C14 is a wonderful testament of our Maker's faithfulness. Although we cannot explain why God is so perfectly holy, His Word and His ways leave no doubt. Why would our Creator give His Own flesh for us? Why would He bear with us so patiently? What significance could the inhabitants of such an infinitesimally small planet have to Him? Why does He care so deeply for us? As the mysteries of nature have no end, so the mysteries of her Author's glorious nature are beyond measure. Still He abides eternally faithful.

C14 also has an even more specific role in honoring the Word of God. It hints at a very young age for the earth. While the thought seems absurd to the Darwinized scientific community, C14 leaves little room on this planet for millions of years. C14 can be harnessed as a powerful tool to date artifacts and natural remains when other means of dating would be difficult or impossible, but it does *not* speak of incredibly long ages.

Beginning in the late 1940s, chemist Willard F. Libby and a small team of researchers set up a system for carbon dating. Libby did not believe the record of reliable ancient Scripture; instead, he believed religiously that millions of years had transpired on our planet. He calculated that the amount of C14 produced by solar radiation each day would naturally balance the amount of C14 that decays in a given day—a state of dynamic equilibrium. According to his calculations it would take less than 30,000 years for our world to initially balance its C14 level. Thus, he assumed that the amount of radiocarbon in the atmosphere during his lifetime was the same as it had been for millions of years.

In order to calibrate their C14 clock, Libby and his team had to compare C14 levels found in artifacts of *known* age. Based on his beliefs, Libby hoped to find a series of measurements that supported a mathematically consistent C14 decay—all beginning with an initial concentration of C14 equal to that observed in Libby's time. He was in for a surprise. C14 seemed to be decaying a little faster than he had expected, most noticeably when measuring things with a known age of more than 2,000 years. But Libby dismissed this trend as an irrelevant factor. The observed C14 concentrations were close enough to his theoretical curve to make a good case for radiocarbon dating. In 1960 Libby won the Nobel Prize for his work.

Today many scientists believe that radiocarbon dating can be used to date objects on earth up to 50,000 years old.[6] But there's a major issue that has been neglected. Further sampling has verified that the world-wide concentration of C14 has been *increasing* over the last 6,000 years. The trend of lower-than-expected C14 concentrations that Libby had dismissed was in fact a relevant detail. Carbon dating must be based on an *initial* C14 to stable carbon ratio. Libby knew this, but he assumed that the global C14 level was balanced and had been balanced for millions of years. We now know that that is *not* the case.

Some of the bristlecone pine trees growing in the American Rocky Mountains are known to be over *4,000 years old* and still living.[7] Each year the trees grow a new layer of vascular tissue that thickens their trunks over time. By looking at the cross section of a tree trunk and counting the annual rings, we can easily determine the age of a given tree. Researchers have carbon dated these growth layers in order to fine-tune their radiocarbon clock.

Secular scientists have had a big part in gathering the radiocarbon data that has *confirmed* the accuracy of reliable ancient Scripture. The marked increase of radiocarbon is very consistent with the biblical record. It appears that thousands of years ago our world was more radioactively clean. The Bible records that at one point the average human life expectancy was several hundred years. Lower radiation levels may have had a big part in those dynamics. The pristine environment of the early earth documented in Scripture is exactly what the results of radiocarbon sampling have suggested. Notwithstanding, the majority of scientists are content to adjust their C14 clock and disregard the cause of discrepancy. It seems we have missed the message.

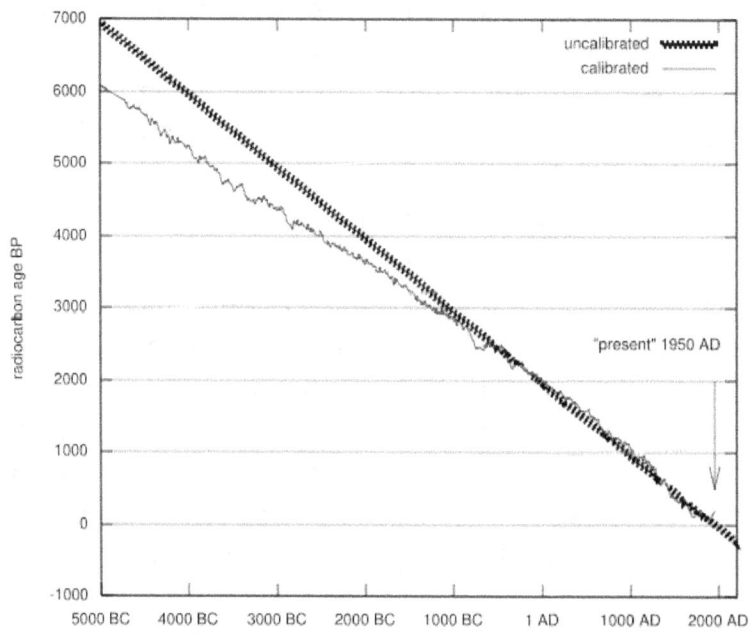

If Libby had respected the authority of Scripture, he would have expected a second curve to influence his model. As our planet approached a dynamic equilibrium, it would gradually curve closer and closer to a final balance of radiocarbon. If this theoretical curve had started at low levels 6,000 years ago, we could calculate its influence on the carbon dating system. This provides a framework for explaining the observed inconsistencies in Libby's model.

But, if radiocarbon was not there to be found 6,000 years ago, what does that do to the radiocarbon dating method? When researchers test a sample that shows practically zero radiocarbon, they assume that the sample is at least 50,000 years old. Yet, the import of Scripture teaches us that such an assumption is skewed. Clean samples could just as well be 6,000 years old as 50,000. Once again, a closer look at the environment explains the misunderstandings of secular men.

Radiocarbon dating is an excellent tool for dating artifacts and natural samples within the timeline defined by Scripture. Trying to imagine our world before that timeframe will always lead to confusion. C14 can be used for a variety of applications, but it is most effective in the real world—not a world of science fiction.

Researchers have worked hard to bring carbon dating into agreement with the real world, but many scientists are still basing their life work on some unrealistic ideas. Not all concepts have been verified as well as radiocarbon dating. For instance, natural selection is among the theories that work much better on paper than in the real world. The ideas behind natural selection are on the whole fairly logical. But when we observe the life cycle of actual species, we are hard pressed to see anything remotely like progressive natural selection at work. Many Darwinists see "survival of the fittest" that occurs as an arms race between predator and prey as the most relevant form of natural selection, and this is the form of natural selection we are discussing here and following.

Darwin said that only the strongest should survive, and Adolf Hitler echoed his thoughts. But in many cases they were both *wrong*. In many cases the weakest survive and the strongest die. In many cases the strong have little opportunity to multiply. This seems to be more an exception than a rule, but it carries with it a powerful wake-up call. If a whole organism with many handicaps can make it through life and have a family, Darwinism has some serious pragmatic issues.

For instance, the Savior (the Strongest) gave His life for the guilty, for the sinful, and for the helpless (the Weakest). He proclaimed a truth displayed in the physical processes of nature. Christ the Messiah from the side of a humble hill in Galilee lifted his voice to an open-air audience and preached:

> Ye have heard that it hath been said, Thou shalt love thy neighbour, and hate thine enemy. But I say unto you, Love your enemies, bless them that curse you, do good to them that hate you, and pray for them which despitefully use you, and persecute you; That ye may be the children of your Father which is in heaven: for he maketh his sun to rise on the evil and on the good, and sendeth rain on the just and on the unjust.[a]

Jehovah provides. Evidence of the goodness of our Creator is scattered throughout the natural world. Even with the dark

---
[a] Matthew 5:43–45

stain of our sin on her, nature experiences God's grace. Jesus continued:

> Behold the fowls of the air: for they sow not, neither do they reap, nor gather into barns; yet your heavenly Father feedeth them. Are ye not much better than they? Which of you by taking thought can add one cubit unto his stature? And why take ye thought for raiment? Consider the lilies of the field, how they grow; they toil not, neither do they spin: And yet I say unto you, That even Solomon in all his glory was not arrayed like one of these. Wherefore, if God so clothe the grass of the field, which to day is, and to morrow is cast into the oven, shall he not much more clothe you, O ye of little faith?[a]

Of course He will. The Author of life knows the needs of life. He supplies our needs as we follow His plan. Faith works. Even in this sin-scarred world, our Maker takes care of sparrows.

Darwin made the imprudent decision to doubt the authority of Scripture, and as a result his ideas were bound for failure. Death and pain are very real factors on this tainted planet, but they do not suffocate life with the kind of force that Darwin imagined. Most of us get plenty of opportunities to breathe—to relax.

The scientific journals contain great volumes about all the concepts of natural selection and its *theoretical* influence on the natural world. But you will be hard-pressed to find good examples of the *real* influence of natural selection in

---

[a] Matthew 6:26–30

action. That is because natural selection is much more of a human ideal than a functional principle of nature. Theories that cannot be proved remain hypothetical ... not factual.

Natural selection depends on individuals who can rise above the crowd. When we see two *species* in conflict with one another—unless certain individuals stand out during the conflict—we are *not* actually witnessing the Darwinistic idea of natural selection. Dawkins[p10] explains:

> [Species-level competition] could account for the pattern of species existing in the world at any particular time. It follows that it could also account for changing patterns of species as geological ages give way to later ages, that is, for changing patterns in the fossil record. But it is not a significant force in the evolution of the complex machinery of life. The most it can do is to choose between various alternative complex machineries, given that those complex machineries have already been put together by true Darwinian selection. As I have put it before, species selection may occur but it doesn't seem to *do* anything much![8]

The pressure of conflict between existing species is too broad to produce finely tuned details in terms of logic. Darwinists place a very great emphasis on very small changes. Those incredibly particular changes must theoretically develop in individuals before spreading to a population. But there's a crucial question. How small do the changes need to be? Well, here is where the Darwinists run into some enormous logical problems.

For Darwinism to seem plausible, the changes that occur on a genetic level would need to be literally undetectable. That is *not* an overstatement. Mutations that can be detected by human investigation are dependably harmful. That is, they destroy things every time. The only way Darwinists can justify their beliefs is by emphasizing invisible changes—changes smaller than any person can recognize. Dawkins finds, "As a matter of fact, virtually all of the mutations studied in genetic laboratories—which are pretty macro because otherwise geneticists wouldn't notice them—are deleterious to the animals possessing them."[9] As a rule, then, those mutations that are macro (having effects large enough to be seen) are also deleterious (harmful to a living thing's health). But notice Dawkins' use of the "macro" clause to soften the crushing blow dealt his favored theory by data collected in the real world.

If *geneticists* cannot recognize the good changes a mutation causes, why should the wild beasts in our world be able to pick out those who don't have the change? If natural selection must rely on such fantastically miniature changes to do anything positive, we should wonder whether the possibility is at all practical. Given these terms we are hard-pressed to find the *utility* of natural selection. A technician working in a laboratory may be able to identify changes within individual cells, but do natural predators actually care that much? And if they do, we can thank our Creator that it is certainly not so in *this* world.

Predators in our world do not use microscopes, yet that is what Darwinism seems to assume. Any mutation that we can *see* is destructive, yet many Darwinists continue to believe that microscopic changes will be systematically identified by natural selection. Dawkins observes: "The chances are very high that a big random jump in genetic space will end in death."[10] He reasons "the smaller the jump the less likely death is, and the more likely is it that the jump will result in improvement.[11]" Darwinistic theory must be built on extremely fine-tuned gradual changes because mathematically there is no other option.

And although the math sounds airtight, at what nanolevel is random improvement reasonable? Would an improvement at such a minute level carry significant weight in a real-world environment? If not, should such a change be classified as a legitimate consequential *improvement* at all? Again, natural predators do not use microscopes to observe prey.

Not only are the units of selection microscopic, but so are also their foreseeable products. Dawkins believes that the "timescale over which significant improvement might be detected is, in any case, likely to be far longer than could be detected by comparing one typical generation with its predecessor."[12] Why should a poor thing's life be at stake over some unnoticeable detail?

What is most remarkable is that evolutionists *know* how generous earth's ecosystems can be. Most of us don't even need both of our lungs to live a healthy life. Dawkins says that life goes on even if our lungs are reduced to one-third of the average capacity. He understands that "death doesn't suddenly arrive below a particular threshold lung area!"[13] His point is that Darwin's intermediates could have theoretically survived in the real world. He cites animals such as flying squirrels as examples. Dawkins argues aggressively that "not only are animals with 'half a wing' common, so are animals with a quarter of a wing."[14] Now, how in this world is natural selection supposed to pick out microscopic details when it allows animals to survive with only quarter of a wing? Quite simply, it does not. Even in its corrupted state, the environment of our world bears the handsome marks of our Maker's grace.

Unfortunately for the Darwinists, however, is the fact that the idea of natural selection has much bigger problems than an unrealistically small target; it also has quite an *assortment* of details to pick through. As we discussed in chapter 3, hidden genetic traits cause an immense number of possible combinations to be available. If a mutation does cause a change, it is very likely that the change could be genetically buried or lost in the second generation. If the mutated genes are not expressed physically, they cannot have selective influence logically. Mayr[p13] clarifies that "any mutation that induces changes in the *phenotype* [emphasis added] will either be favored or discriminated against by natural selection."[15] A phenotype is the actual body that is expressed by genes. Logic demands that the idea of natural selection cannot use traits that remain hidden. Natural selection is, in fact, utterly impotent to remove most recessive traits (e.g. albino plants).

The principle of vanishing mutations is only an appetizer on the banquet table among an assortment of selection issues that genetic cycles cause. We understand that no two people are alike, but what does that imply for the idea of natural selection? If one of us develops a microscopic advantage, its significance will be greatly influenced by our overall physical makeup. Since our overall physical makeup will always be noticeably different from that of our children, the significance of a microscopic advantage will fluctuate intensely through the generations.

If undetectably small mutations are like finding a needle in a haystack, then genetic cycles imply that the haystack—where the needle may or may not be—is constantly rearranged. It's one thing to imagine selection finding the same needle in the same haystack for several generations, but it is quite another to imagine selection taking the time to sort through millions of generations of *different* haystacks. This kind of hard-working natural selection fits better in science fiction novels than it does in serious scientific discussion.

In our world natural selection cannot do what Darwinists want it to do. Death is not a precise pressure; it is the consequence of our spiritual wrongdoing. Death is an ugly brute that is not serving to progress nature. It is, rather, a deep scar on the face of our Creator's work.

Our environment eliminates the logical possibility of certain ideas. Although death is not much of a technician, it is perhaps one of the starkest events in our world. Reliable ancient Scripture cautions, "It is appointed unto men once to die, but after this the judgment."[a] Death comes to the young and to the old, to the rich and to the poor, to the simple-minded and to the intellectual, to the unsightly and to the lovely, to the unknown and to the well-known. It does not follow simple rules, and it will not respect our wishes. But when we see death strike others, we are challenged to find truth; we are reminded that there is a reality Keeper; we are stirred to recognize the limits of the human mind. Death illustrates the principle of natural parameters quite well.

The setting of this world executes and properly lays to rest the arrogant ideas of ungodly souls. Before the human invention of the wheel, God's people understood that God abides outside of nature and that nature is His *work*. The Creator of nature is not the product of natural laws. Rather

---

[a] Hebrews 9:27

natural laws are the product of His wisdom. By contrast, natural science *must* submit to the laws of nature because it is based solely upon them. This logic is readily accessible, yet many brilliant scientists refuse to receive it.

God is not the product of nature; nature is the product of God. Pigliucci[p6] will not accept this fact. He complains, "It is simply unfair."[16] He feels that the second law of thermodynamics should not be applied to Darwinism, unless it can be applied to the Creator as well. Atheists often use this illogical line of reasoning. If atheists, however, want to believe that the universe built itself using the existing laws of nature, then that is *their* problem. Christians discern that God *made* the laws in the first place. We are not obligated to explain His existence based on the natural laws that He authored. As a rule, the most respected men throughout history have recognized the truth of this point, and a few highly distinguished scientists still do.[17]

In this world we are limited in the distance we can drive a golf ball or the speed at which we can run. In the fields of science certain limits cannot be avoided. Science will not tell us how the universe began; it will not tell us what life means; it will not heal our souls. In the 1960s Lindsey[p12] wrote: "We have increased in technology so rapidly in the past few years.... However, all the educational advances have not brought mankind one step further towards solving the basic needs of love, security, and true happiness; on the contrary, civilization seems more removed from these concepts than ever."[18] The culture of the early 21st century goes a long way in confirming Lindsey's sentiment.

Zealous secular scientists are writing checks on science that the truth of natural and social laws will not cash, and our culture has now been left holding a large pile of them voided and returned. Many people are looking for answers that science cannot provide. In a chapter titled "The Future of Happiness" Harris[p19] remarks: "Some of what psychologists have learned about human well-being confirms what everyone already knows: people tend to be happier if they have good friends, basic control over their lives, and enough money to meet their needs."[19] A truly sad testament to the futile end of secular reasoning is that Harris' own book attempts to shut the door on the first two of these. He believes that all kindness is selfishness in disguise and that free will is an absolute illusion. Basically Harris has left us with money as our sole hope, and many of those who *have* money can testify that it is overrated. So much for "the future of happiness."[a]

Thanks to the Author of life, the world that Harris has described is not the end of our hope. We really can have friends who care about us sincerely, and we do have an authentically free will. These, however, are not—as many have thought—the most important matters affecting our personal needs. Our greatest need is *spiritual* healing. While science is a genuinely remarkable tool, it cannot meet that need. Only one Person can meet that need. That Person is Jesus Christ.[b] He is the Messiah of which the Old Testament prophesied so frequently. And He is the Savior of all who accept His gift.[c] That is Good News for anyone who has been looking this world over.

---

[a] Ecclesiastes 5:10
[b] Psalm 103:3; 147:3; Isaiah 53:5; 1 Peter 2:24
[c] Romans 5:17-18; 6:23

IMPLICATION

Here comes the bride all dressed in white! The ushers have just extended a long clean runner down the center aisle, and suddenly everyone in the room rises in honor—as a stunning figure enters. Through the back doors of the auditorium, a lady in snow-white attire and of robust complexion floods the room with her purely energizing presence. In mere moments she stands by a rapt young man, and together they enter a new covenant. With two round metal bands close by, they voice words of profound devotion.

The setting in which we live conveys very specific implications. In a traditional Christian wedding each part of the ceremony expresses an exact message. The white dress speaks of the bride's moral purity; the clean runner, of her unsullied way; the standing audience, of her unspoiled value; and the round metal bands, of a strong and endless love. Even the bride and groom themselves are figurative—symbolizing the local church and Christ, her Redeemer. And while the underlying messages in the natural world are not as artificially staged as they are in such a wedding, they are present.

All the cultures of the world share certain truths. It is, in fact, normal for us to have a strong sense of what is right, even though we frequently fail to *act* on our consciences. Mayr[p13] agrees: "The cultures of the Christian world do have ethical principles that are, on the whole, perfectly sound, even though we have failed so often to follow them."[20] Natural courses of events have a way of educating us if we are paying attention. The second part of Psalm 9:16 reveals that "the wicked is snared in the work of his own hands." Nature has a way of proving her Author's points. The many parables used throughout the Gospels remind us that the natural world is embedded with almost endless lessons.

As individuals we will have differences of opinion, and we are entitled to them; yet all of us are conscious of certain truths that do not lend themselves to multiple opinions. This is not to say that we would all *openly* agree in those areas, but that we are all *aware* of certain truths at a personal core level. For instance, although everyone knows instinctively that gender has inherent meaning, many have to a serious degree convinced themselves otherwise and would argue passionately that it is subject to preference. [a] Gender is sacred—as evidenced by nearly every cell of the body. There is a reason that two people of the same gender will never naturally produce children. If we will be reasonable, we would all admit that nature often offers us more truth than we have garnered from it.

Human decisions are powerful, but they cannot negate the revelations of nature. We need to lead our culture in rediscovering the virtue of responsibility. Harris[p19] asks, "Would you cease to love your child if you learned that he or she was gay?"[21] People who commit homosexual acts do not somehow become "gay," they are just common people who can find new hope and a better way in the Person of Jesus Christ. We ought *always* to care for others regardless of the circumstances—the Scripture commands it.[b] Our love and concern for people, however, does not justify harmful behaviors—in fact, doing so would be an uncaring and unloving act. At no point should we cease to show concern for

---

[a] Genesis 2:24; Leviticus 18:22; Matthew 19:4-5; Romans 1:22-27
[b] Matthew 5:44, Luke 6:27, 35

the well-being of others;[a] but true well-being is *spiritual,* and it will always be the byproduct of doing right in the sight of our Creator. To care for others effectively, we must steer them toward right behaviors—behaviors prescribed in Scripture.

Nature's essence provides an extensive curriculum of spiritual lessons. Christians who believe Scripture do not need to fight and fuss to prove points. There is a truth Keeper who will not be moved by people's opinions—however artfully couched. We can trust His ability and *rest* confidently in it. Believers *should* work to help those who have gone astray, but there is no need to use force—all the power of eternity is already behind the truth. It is the responsibility of believers to make that truth more accessible; sometimes through sharp, compassion-motivated, personal confrontation, but *never* through bullying or physical aggression.

A vast assortment of the world's misguided religious systems parts ways with true Christianity at this point. *Every* unhealthy religion on this globe is based on *human* potential. Many of such are built on a more or less balanced combination of human power and virtue, and the remainder lean heavily on human virtue. The first of these two classifications often misguide by a focus on the extraordinary abilities of men and women. These systems usually stress all that an individual can *do* through the power of self-controlled determination, and will often use force to accomplish their ends. Bulldog religions of this sort flourish because they harness the ungodly power of pride and train people to discipline themselves—resulting in improved levels of physical achievement.

---

[a] 1 Corinthians 13:4–8

The fanatical worship of athletes (the word "fan" is short for fanatic) is among the stealthiest and most widely destructive of these religions in the West. Churchgoers will blow off church meetings to attend sporting events on the Lord's day. Grown men and women often attend church services itching to get *out* and pour themselves into their lord and master. The legs and muscle tone of baseball, basketball, hockey, soccer, and football players have become a primary focus of American idolatry. Playing games can be a good form of recreation, but it is a weak cause to live for.

Bulldog religions produce results, but they are not honest. Many groups have fought mercilessly to gain religious influence through the years. Geisler[p34] recounts: "After a brief but unfruitful attempt to propagate his faith peacefully, Mohammed turned to military force to spread Islam."[22] By following this pattern throughout the years, many have experienced a form of success. Their greatest concern has not been spiritual honesty, but rather self-righteousness and physical control. The list of such groups is almost endless.

In fact, several groups that would fall under a dictionary definition of "Christian" are simply bulldogs with a deceptive alias. They trust "many wonderful works," but the Lord Jesus has never known them![a] Many have standardized a humanistic Roman-military form of "Christianity." Those who think too much of their abilities will tend to take too heavy a burden along their way. These people hope to shoulder the vast weight of their sin but lose their spirit under the load.

Honesty invites the Savior's relieving influence like nothing else will. When we learn to speak the Spirit's language,

---

[a] Matthew 7:22-23

He hears and *whisks* us along. Isaiah prophesied that "Even the youths shall faint and be weary, and the young men shall utterly fall: But they that wait upon the LORD shall renew their strength; they shall mount up with wings as eagles; they shall run, and not be weary; and they shall walk, and not faint."[a] Godly honesty expresses itself in humility and finds the power of God as nothing else can.[b]

Nature tells us that humility is honest. *Our Creator has no need of our strength.* He will allow us to have a part in His work, but that is our privilege not His need. We intuitively know that humility is honest by observing the natural world. The power that is on display before us is beyond measure. The total combined strength of humanity throughout its history is less than a trifling blip on the ageless power meter of nature.

"In the beginning *God.*"[c] The universe is our Maker's handiwork; and, as such, it is an expression of who He is. The Almighty is Jehovah—the self-existent One.[d] His power has no limits, and He has *never* needed anything … ever. While rapt in the Spirit of the Almighty, the Apostle John announced, "Thou art worthy, O Lord, to receive glory and honour and power: for thou hast created all things, and for thy pleasure they are and were created."[e] For His pleasure, nature is spread before our senses. He does as He pleases, and He does all things very *well.*

"In the beginning God *created the heaven and the earth.*"[f] All at *once* the substance—the energy—of the entire

---

[a] Isaiah 40:30–31
[b] James 4:6
[c] Genesis 1:1 (Emphasis added.)
[d] Exodus 6:3
[e] Revelation 4:11
[f] Genesis 1:1 (Emphasis added.)

physical universe was allocated for the purpose. The amount of energy was particular and purposeful. The Creator had no shortages and no second thoughts. In that one moment all of the power displayed in nature was settled—paid in full.

"In the beginning God created the heaven and the earth. *And the earth was without form and void.*"[a] All the energy of the universe was in an unstable form. There was no solid matter. There were no features. Everything was an apportioned quantity of energy. Nature was a fluid formless mass.

"In the beginning God created the heaven and the earth. And the earth was without form, and void; *and darkness was upon the face of the deep.*"[b] Nature revealed nothing because it was unlit, fluid and featureless. Yet, the power that was present was deep—vast and impressive. Only it could not be seen in such a form. It could not be appreciated. It was unrevealed.

"In the beginning God created the heaven and the earth. And the earth was without form, and void; and darkness was upon the face of the deep. And *the Spirit of God moved upon the face of the waters.*"[c] When the Spirit of God stirs fluid materials, those fluid materials have a solid future ahead of them.

"In the beginning God created the heaven and the earth. And the earth was without form, and void; and darkness was upon the face of the deep. And the Spirit of God moved upon the face of the waters. And *God said, Let there be*

---

[a] Genesis 1:1–2 (Emphasis added.)
[b] Genesis 1:1–2a (Emphasis added.)
[c] Genesis 1:1–2 (Emphasis added.)

light."[a] Our Maker speaks from His heart. In the heart of our Creator is a desire to make the obscure clear; to make the cloudy bright. He loves to reveal truth to those who will appreciate it.

"In the beginning God created the heaven and the earth. And the earth was without form, and void; and darkness was upon the face of the deep. And the Spirit of God moved upon the face of the waters. And God said, Let there be light: *and there was light.*"[b] There was light, but no created light sources. God was the direct source of light. The last chapter of Scripture teaches us that God's city will be lit this way. It reveals, "And there shall be no night there; and they need no candle, neither light of the sun; for the Lord God giveth them light: and they shall reign for ever and ever."[c] The essence of God radiates light.

There was light, but what was it? Perhaps it was *everything*. The knowledge of God is without limit. Psalm 147:5 exclaims, "Great is our Lord, and of great power: his understanding is infinite."[d] Stars were not yet formed, and still there was light, like a visual blueprint of all that *would* be. The light itself was created waiting for the substance that would be behind it. God had revealed—ahead of time—His plan for nature. He knows where He is going. "For I know the thoughts that I think toward you, saith the LORD, thoughts of peace, and not of evil, to give you an expected end."[e] The same pattern can be seen throughout Scripture. Our Shepherd often

---

[a] Genesis 1:1-3a (Emphasis added.)
[b] Genesis 1:1-3 (Emphasis added.)
[c] Revelation 22:5
[d] Psalm 147:5
[e] Jeremiah 29:11

THE SETTING: IMPLICATION   169

gives light first and the full balance in His own time. We trust that "Faithful is he that calleth you, who also will do it."[a]

With a fully-dimensional physical blueprint of the universe in place, God *stretched* out the universe. We know that "he ... created the heavens, and stretched them out;"[b] that His "hands, have stretched out the heavens;"[c] that He "stretched forth the heavens, and laid the foundations of the earth;"[d] and that He "stretched out the heavens by his discretion."[e] All the raw material was present and the plan was in place. Then He *did* it. By His Word and that power our Creator placed the mass of the universe. Through at least 20 billion light years of space, it appears that our Maker supernaturally pulled the mass of the universe near light speed—He ran time through the rest of the universe as if it were *backwards*!

During one ordinary 24-hour day on earth, most of the lifeless universe experienced billions of years. Though that might seem awkward from our perspective, in physics time is relative to speed. Reliable ancient Scripture exposes the fact that the earth is less than 7,000 years old. We know this based on the specific language and the human genealogies that the Bible records. Time on earth, however, is not necessarily the same as time in the rest of the universe. In fact, on a cosmic level, matching timeframes are quite *sparse*.

With astronomical data increasing in recent decades, astrophysicists have identified a major contradiction. As far as science can tell, light is faster than anything else in the

---

[a] 1 Thessalonians 5:24
[b] Isaiah 42:5
[c] Isaiah 45:12
[d] Isaiah 51:13
[e] Jeremiah 10:12

observable universe. And although galaxies can be seen across 20 billion light years of space, most astrophysicists believe that the universe must be less than 20 billion years old. Many see this as an impossible discrepancy.[23] If the light was in place *before* anything else, however, there is no challenge. We just need to believe the Word that we have. Nature presents no conflict here, just immense power.

Our Creator is not impressed by human abilities, and nature lets us know that. We really don't even need to look far to get a hit of the power that nature has on display. Einstein's mass/energy equivalence equation—$E=mc^2$—defines energy in terms of mass. Everything in our world is built of energy. The wisdom of God has converted much of the fluid energy of nature into *solid mass*. Every solid thing that we handle speaks of fierce, pride-zapping power. Greene[p9] illustrates: "From $E=mc^2$, we know that mass and energy are interchangeable; like dollars and euros, they are convertible currencies (but unlike monetary currencies, they have a fixed exchange rate, given by the speed of light times itself, c^2)."[24] Having a conversion factor of c^2 means that great amounts of energy are represented by even a little mass.

Mass includes some energy that cannot be weighed, but as a general rule, 454 grams of mass equal 1 pound under normal conditions on the earth's surface. Based on this relationship we can evaluate the minimum amount of energy represented by objects of a given weight. Our sun uses nuclear fusion to convert subatomic particles of hydrogen into radiation energy, and it is a very efficient system. Greene calculates, "The sun's life-sustaining heat and light are generated by the conversion of 4.3 million tons of matter into energy every second."[25] That may seem like a large amount of matter, but the earth absorbs only 1 part out of 2,160,000,000 parts of energy emitted by the sun. That means that less than five *pounds* of matter are used for the *earth* each second.[26]

We can limit our target even more to draw out a very familiar illustration. Given that the sun heats the earth with only a few pounds of matter per second, how much energy does the sun use to heat New York City? New York City covers about 305 square miles, which is less than 0.0006% of the earth's solar footprint.[27] This means that New York City's environment is heated with less than *19 ounces* of matter per 12-hour day!

While that seems remarkably efficient, more solar mass than we would suspect is either absorbed by the earth's upper atmosphere or otherwise lost in conversion (so that its effects are not directly felt near the earth's surface). In fact, a single ounce of ordinary mass represents *700,000 megawatt hours* of energy.[28]

On July 22, 2011, the New York City energy grid was strained as residents tried to keep themselves cool. The power consumption spiked briefly to 13,200 megawatts. If the power output had remained at this dangerous level for 48 hours, all the energy necessary could have been found in 1 *ounce* of ordinary mass with juice to spare![29] Under normal circumstances New York is one of the most efficient cities in the United States.[30] On average the mass of your typical half-ounce plastic *toothbrush* could power the Big Apple for about 60 hours.[31]

A proper understanding of nature can dramatically improve spiritual hygiene. Psalm 19 celebrates that "the heavens declare the glory of God"; and as the sciences mature, we are learning that just about everything else does too. The creation speaks of her Creator, and her message is clear and resounding. Every day the word goes out. We know that

"There is no speech nor language, where their voice is not heard."[a] The voice of nature is potent and univocal.

As we understand nature more deeply, we find more reasons to respect the Creator more reverently. No one knows what the parts of an atom really consist of, but many have proffered educated guesses during the last few years. We call subatomic particles electrons, quarks, neutrinos, and other names, and we have a *general* description of what they are. Yet—to date—no one understands what these super microscopic particles actually *are*. Several of the developing theories regarding this question could have magnificent implications. A personal favorite is string theory.

String theory holds that all the fundamental particles of the natural world are produced by the vibration of übermicroscopic strings. Greene[p9] notes: "The *mass* of a particle in string theory is nothing but the *energy* of its vibrating string." He continues: "All the properties that we use to distinguish one particle from another are determined by the vibrational pattern of the particle's string."[32] While string theory is still quite hypothetical, it presents a beautiful possibility.

We know that nature broadcasts a message of our Creator's greatness and "day unto day uttereth speech,"[b] but it may well be that it does so in an unimaginably wonderful way. Could it be that strings, like innumerable vocal cords, raise their voice in worship of the Creator? Greene—as a secular physicist—suggests, "At the ultramicroscopic level, the universe would be akin to a string symphony vibrating matter into existence."[33] When David penned the words of his Creator in Psalm 19, and when he addressed those words to

---

[a] Psalm 19:3
[b] Psalm 19:2

the Chief Musician, he probably wasn't thinking of the "speech" of physically embedded vocal cords; but if string theory is right, Someone else was.

An interesting sidebar is that one of the most popular versions of string theory suggests six unknown dimensions and time that the strings vibrate through.[34] That would give a total of *seven* dimensions that are beyond our physical control. By no means is string theory to be confused with verified reliable science, but its implications make good food for thought.

Nature speaks of God. We can hear a voice of power and of wisdom. The language is vibrant and distinct, and we need not doubt the message. All that we have points to the accuracy of reliable ancient Scripture. It is awkward and dishonest to deny the inference. When Darwin began turning from Scripture and instead defending his godless ideals, he developed heart palpitations and had disturbing dreams.[35] Nature presents truth too often for us to refuse it in good conscience. Dawkins[p10] observes: "Our brains seem predisposed to resist Darwinism."[36] Not only are our brains predisposed to resist it, but all of nature detests such irresponsibility.

Dawkins hopes that having the presence of thought to resist Darwinism is a simple misunderstanding. He says that since we can design complex systems intelligently, we infer that the massive complexity of the universe was also *intelligently* designed. Dawkins literally recommends a "leap of the imagination" to rid ourselves of the nagging perception of a universe Designer—a perception that has been deeply engraven upon the human soul. Dawkins openly admits that the ultimate goal of his book *The Blind Watchmaker* is "to help the reader to make this leap."[37] But the urge to reject Darwinism is not a simple misfire of the human brain; we reject Darwinism because we cannot seem to shake off reality—beginning with the logical statement, which has been verified countless times by empirical observation, that *everything that had a beginning had a cause*. So, could we, the most complex organisms in the known universe, be an accident—merely animated dirt? The human mind simply *knows* better!

Indeed, the human mind is a frail tool; but when it is functioning well, we have a powerful capacity to taste the essence of a definite reality. And, frankly, it is unacceptable to conclude that a fortunate turn of events has finally allowed matter to become aware of itself after untold eons of unconsciousness. Someone sees what no earthly eye sees. Someone knows what no human mind knows. At some level, we each find that to be conscious of reality is to be conscious of the reality Keeper.

Who's keeping track of everything? Nature does not have to behave itself as far as science is concerned. Pigliucci[p6] finds that "there is no a priori reason why the world should behave logically and predictably, but apparently it does."[38] The phrase "a priori" roughly means "built-in." In other words, there is no built-in reason for Nature to follow discrete rules. Every particle of nature is sustained and ordered by the power and wisdom of God. He keeps account of every detail of the universe.

Some religions emphasize human potential based primarily on humanistic *virtue*. They do not so much shove or bite like the bulldogs but rather float like delicate butterflies. These religious systems harness the ungodly power of subtle lies to soften all the edges of truth. In their minds they blend themselves with God. In the softest and most gradual manner possible, they degrade the Creator. They function in a world of gray and imagine that the Author of reality does not keep hard-and-fast records—that there is no need for Messiah's blood to be shed. They are tragically mistaken.

Such butterflies do not learn to take sin seriously because they trust in their own good nature to preserve them, and as a result they never come clean.[a] They live blurred and dirty lives—always in love with nature, but never revering the power and justice that its essence conveys. The Hindu, Shinto, Buddhist, and other—primarily eastern—religious systems fall into this category. In addition to these, a large number of such religious systems that would be loosely classified as "Christian" also fall into this category. These deceptive and poisonous butterflies have "ministries of encouragement" but leave spiritual cancers unaddressed. And, in so doing, they serve to embolden those in error, slandering the name of Christ. The blood of Christ needs to be *preached* again.[b] If we fail to take sin seriously, we will fail to search out help, and we will rot from the inside out.

Jesus Christ gave His life so that we can have life. He pleads today with those who are lost and wandering. To the parched soul the Lord Jesus calls out, "If any man thirst, let him come unto me, and drink."[c] We need a thirst for truth. As long as we are consumed with justifying ourselves, we will not develop a desire for our Creator's cosmic level of righteousness and will thus doom ourselves to living in a gray yin-yang fog. The Apostle Paul weeps, "Brethren, my heart's desire and prayer to God for Israel is, that they might be saved. For I bear them record that they have a zeal of God, but not according to

---

[a] Romans 3:23; 5:12
[b] Ephesians 1:7; Colossians 1:14; Hebrews 9:12,14; 1 John 1:8
[c] John 7:37

knowledge. For they being ignorant of God's righteousness, and going about to establish their own righteousness, have not submitted themselves unto the righteousness of God."[a] Those who try to "establish their own righteousness" will not—and *cannot* in such an attempt—"submit to the righteousness of God."

Highbrow critics often lampoon Bible-believers as if Christians were all dull-minded rednecks. Harris[p19] even goes so far as to insist that salvation and spiritual rebirth are forms of mental *suicide*. He flaunts his spiritual arrogance like a banner and rallies a pride-poisoned following with it. But the simplicity of Scripture reveals wisdom that humanism cannot accept. In the pages of Scripture we learn of laws that humble us—laws that profoundly dwarf every field of science. The wisdom of God is in no contest with a few ounces of gray matter between a person's ears.[b] The more we genuinely understand, the less we get high on ourselves, and the more we emphasize the greatness of our Maker. If we hope to understand science, we would do well first to recognize the Source of all the consistencies that make science possible.

Isaac Newton had a fair grasp of how significant his own place in nature was. He had a key role in the development of *multiple* sciences. He *discovered* gravity, the three laws of motion, and many central principles of visible light. He also *invented* several key methods of mathematics including calculus. He reminisced: "I do not know what I may appear to the world; but to myself I seem to have been only like a boy playing on the seashore, and diverting myself in now and then finding a smoother pebble or a prettier shell

---

[a] Romans 10:1-3
[b] Romans 11:33

than ordinary, whilst the great ocean of truth lay all undiscovered before me."[39] As a man with such profound understanding of the natural world, Newton was awed by it. He was a man who respected his Creator deeply and reflected that sense of respect as a mathematician and scientist.

While Newton's sense of reverence for the Creator has grown scarce among scientists in recent years, there are still a few highly distinguished experts who are believers. Francis Collins is, at the time of this writing, the director of the National Institutes of Health (NIH) and the former head of the Human Genome Project. He is a highly-trained scientist who has greater influence over medical research than anyone else on our planet, and he is a professing Christian. What is quite remarkable about Collins is his concept of natural history—he is a *Darwinist*. Collins was instructed by Darwinistic professors and still believes that Darwinism is acceptable science. Collins was spiritually convicted about his own sin and recognized his personal need of a Savior simply by studying *nature*. He believes that if nature is ordered enough to allow evolution, nature *must* have a divinely wise Creator. Even though the Scripture does not fit Collins' full concept of natural history, the implications of nature were too powerful for Collins to reject their import. Apparently he does not recognize the conflicts between Darwinism and Scripture; but it seems that he got nature's basic message, and that is what counts for his eternity—he professes to have trusted Jesus Christ as his personal Savior.

We have absolutely no excuse to doubt the testimony of the natural world. Rejecting the collective witness of nature is not a matter of misunderstanding but of willful rebellion. All the necessary information is before us, we need only to admit its relevance. If we think too highly of our abilities, we set ourselves up for disastrous consequences.[a] In order to understand where we fit in nature, we need to consult with our Designer. As we soak in *His* counsel, we will grow deep and healthy roots.[b] Academic growth without a corresponding *spiritual* growth is top-heavy; it has a pitiful base, and it topples under any real weight. Knowledge without spiritual maturity results in impressive facades concealing no substance; it goes with every wind and crumbles along the way. We cannot afford a spiritually gaunt scientific community that will yield on weak results. We need to *respect* our setting for what it is—a simple word of wisdom.

---

[a] Romans 12:3
[b] Psalm 33:11; Proverbs 19:21

RELEVANCE

We need desperately to be put in our place. As we peer intently into the reflecting pool surrounding us, reality surfaces.[a] In those ever-present waters we can discover the truth of our Creator's Word about us. In turn, the power of that godly honesty propels personal and scientific achievement beyond all common parameters while, at the same time, yielding a level of spiritual satisfaction that spurns all the fads and merchandise of secular logic.

All spiritual truth is footed squarely at the feet of the Savior. The Holy Spirit of God meets us there and equips us with genuine humility. Along our way to that place of refuge, however, we see the street signs lit with the neon of our Creator's work. Still, only through the optic of godly sincerity can we see clearly amid the smokescreens of overblown opinions and humanistic theories based not on science but on the desire to be free of the Author and the Truth of His Word.

Nature—when viewed in proper focus—has a wonderful tendency to put us in our place; the human bent, however, will always soil the lens of honesty with godless pride. The public spotlight can blind us to relevant objects a certain distance from us. When we think too much of ourselves, we leave little space to discover the rest of the cosmos. The Author of consciousness deserves our selfless attention. He is the focal point, the Center, around which nature is assembled. To understand science, we must first orient it properly relative to *Him*. The reason we disregard our Maker is that we hope to usurp His position as Ruler of the

---

[a] James 1:23-25

universe. The result is an anemic, scraggy form of pseudo-science that leaves us confused and wanting.

We have more than enough information available. What we need is *honesty* to appreciate what we have. When we refuse the light that our Teacher delivers openly to us, we are consigning ourselves to a lifetime in the dark. Jesus exposes that "light is come into the world, and men loved darkness rather than light, because their deeds were evil."[a] Our sin is *real*, and we need real forgiveness for it. The more we bury our wrong, the more confusing our world becomes. We cannot evaluate nature accurately if we allow spiritual dirt at a personal level; all our instruments of logic will produce skewed or discolored readings. So in the end the future of accurate science is threatened by the same poison that damns souls for eternity—sin.

At some point each of us needs to come to terms with our spiritual dirt and needs. We cannot appropriately shoulder the burden of discerning between right and wrong nor reliably *do* what we feel *is* right—for every pain in our world stems from souls who thought they could. Jesus warned, "Take heed therefore that the light which is in thee be not darkness."[b] Humanistic morality is hazardously deceptive. We need a godly heart and the eternal wisdom God provides more than we let on; the natural events of life and nature herself tell us this.

Jesus Christ humbled Himself for our sakes.[c] He made Himself one of us and gave His life to bring us forgiveness. His body was fastened to a cross with nails driven through the

---

[a] John 3:19
[b] Luke 11:35
[c] Philippians 2:5-11

base of his hands and through the muscles of His feet, yet it was His *compassion* for us that held Him there.[a] A wreath made of thorny branches was beaten into the Savior's scalp, but beneath that crown of thorns the burden of *our* sins was on His mind and heart.[b] He shouldered what we could not; He carried the weight of our sins. This event—the crucifixion of Jesus Christ that is utter foolishness to many of the "learned" members of the science community—is in fact the central event of all history. Just before His death, our Redeemer pronounced the greatest message that has ever graced the natural world: "It is finished."[c] The price for our sins had been paid; all the work that we could not do had been done for us.

Today each of us comes to a simple crossroads. What we do with the Word of God determines everything meaningful in our lives. The choice is clear: We can either accept His work and learn from His wisdom or continue toward our own dead end. The Hope of this world is not *of* us, but He can live *within* us. He has finished the work and risen in triumph. The truth is before us; we need not search far. Any one of us—from any background whatsoever—can immediately become spiritually clean through the blood of the Lamb.[d]

Romans 10:12-13 assures us that "there is no difference between the Jew and the Greek: for the same Lord over all is rich unto all that call upon him. For whosoever shall call upon the name of the Lord shall be saved." When we believe the Word of God, we will no longer try to justify ourselves.[e] We

---

[a] Psalm 78:38
[b] Matthew 27:29
[c] John 19:30
[d] 1 Peter 1:18-19
[e] Romans 3:23

will recognize ourselves as sinners, and *this* will motivate us to call out for salvation.[a] The whole cost has already been paid, in full, but tragically too many have refused the free gift.[b] Ungodly pride locks us up to die in a prison of spiritual despair and disease, while the Great Physician waits with open arms to receive us. If you never have before, please pray and accept Jesus Christ as your personal Savior.

The life of faith is life as it was meant to be. All the bedrock that we need is within reach; the invitation is open. "And the Spirit and the bride say, Come. And let him that heareth say, Come. And let him that is athirst come. And whosoever will, let him take the water of life freely."[c] When the Word of God lays the foundation, this life is not so muddy after all. Take the simple gift—it's the only way to live.

---

[a] Romans 5:8
[b] Romans 6:23
[c] Revelation 22:17

CHAPTER 5 REVIEW

STUDY NOTE: This final chapter examines the actual location and dimensions in which human life resides. Regardless of how surreal life can seem at times, we are all actually here on this little planet in the Milky Way. Many philosophical theories seem plausible, but often in the real world they are found to be frankly wrong. Our natural setting is restrictive, yet provides an immense feast of implications to humble us and reveal to us the relevance of the whole matter. Here may well be the most pointed and practical subject of our study. (See pages 207-210 for suggested answers)

THE JURISDICTION OF THE SETTING:
1. How did Alan Shepard easily one-arm a golf ball over 300 yards?
2. What is the difference between reasonable concepts and realistic ones?
3. What did Isaiah prophecy would be the heritage of the Lord's servants?
4. What does Harris believe the good life is all about?
5. How long will it take for half a sample of C14 to become stable nitrogen?
6. How long would C14 need to decay to 1/8 an original concentration?
7. What is dynamic equilibrium as it applies to earth's C14?
8. From no C14 to dynamic equilibrium how long would it take on earth?
9. Carbon dating samples of known age reveals what about earth's history?
10. Why must carbon dating be based on an <u>initial</u> C14 to stable carbon ratio?
11. What do Darwinists see as the most relevant form of natural selection?
12. Why would natural selection have to be very particular to be progressive?
13. Why are Darwinists obligated to trust in invisible genetic mutations?
14. If mutations must accumulate for many generations before they become a survival factor, how would small mutations differ from large?
15. How does death illustrate the principle of natural parameters?
16. Why do natural laws apply to natural sciences, yet not to God?
17. How does Harris deny the possibility of what he considers two key qualifications for happiness?
18. What is the greatest personal need of every human being?

THE IMPLICATION OF THE SETTING:

1. Who said, "The cultures of the Christian world do have ethical principles that are, on the whole, perfectly sound, even though we have failed so often to follow them"?
2. What Bible passage infers natural events will prove God's way right?
3. What teaching method often used by Jesus Christ shows that nature is embedded with almost endless life lessons?
4. How do people know that gender has meaning?
5. Why is it futile to argue against truth?
6. What is a very stealthy and destructive "bulldog" religion in the West?
7. What pattern have Muslims used with great success?
8. In what way are some so-called Christian groups "bulldogs" at heart?
9. How does godly honesty lead to humility?
10. What are some ways that the universe expresses its Designer?
11. What is the meaning of "darkness was upon the face of the deep"?
12. What does God's first quote "Let there be light" tell us about Him?
13. Genesis 1:3 says "there was light," but what was it?
14. If the earth is less than 7,000 years old, how can parts of the universe be over 14 billion years old?
15. What does having a conversion factor of c^2 mean in $E=mc^2$?
16. Can the sun heat New York City for 12 hours using 19 ounces of matter?
17. What theory proposes that the fundamental particles of the natural world are produced by the vibration of extremely small strings?
18. Who said that if string theory were correct "the universe would be akin to a string symphony vibrating matter into existence"?
19. Who said, "Our brains seem predisposed to resist Darwinism"?
20. What is strongly implied by an orderly and predictable universe?
21. Why do "butterflies" see no need for Messiah's blood to be shed?
22. Why is it impossible for some to "submit to the righteousness of God"?
23. What great scientist defined himself "like a boy playing on the seashore"?
24. Why did Francis Collins trust Christ as his personal Savior?

THE RELEVANCE OF THE SETTING:

1. In what way will spiritual satisfaction spurn the fads of secular logic?
2. Why is spiritual truth found exclusively at the feet of Christ?
3. Why is most the universe invisible from earth during daylight hours?
4. What does the Author of consciousness logically deserve?
5. Why does good science need to be oriented around the Creator?
6. Why do people tend to reject spiritual light when it is made available?
7. How does sin threaten the future of accurate science?
8. What is the gravest danger of sin?
9. What is the central event of all history?
10. What was finished when Jesus Christ said "It is finished"?
11. How does believing the Bible put an end to self-righteousness?
12. How is the gift of eternal salvation received?

APPENDIX
365 Messianic Prophecies
Jewish Scripture prophecies *fulfilled* by the life of Jesus Christ

Genesis 3:15	Seed of a woman /virgin birth...Luke 1:35; Matthew 1:18-20
Genesis 3:15	He will bruise Satan's head...Hebrews 2:14; 1 John 3:18
Genesis 5:24	The bodily ascension to heaven illustrated...Mark 6:19
Genesis 9:26-27	The God of Shem will be the Son of Shem...Luke 3:36
Genesis 12:3	As Abraham's seed, will bless all nations...Acts 3:25,26
Genesis 12:7	The Promise made to Abraham's Seed....Galatians 3:16
Genesis 14:18	A priest after Melchizedek...Hebrews 6:20
Genesis 14:18	A King also...Hebrews 7:2
Genesis 14:18	The Last Supper foreshadowed....Matthew 26:26-29
Genesis 17:19	The Seed of Isaac......Romans. 9:7
Genesis 21:12	Seed of Isaac...Romans 9:7; Hebrews 11:18
Genesis 22:8	The Lamb of God promised....John 1:29
Genesis 22:18	As Isaac's seed, will bless all nations....Galatians 3:16
Genesis 26:2-5	The Seed of Isaac promised as the Redeemer...Hebrews11:18
Genesis 49:10	The time of His coming....Luke 2:1-7; Galatians 4:4
Genesis 49:10	The Seed of Judah......Luke 3:33
Genesis 49:10	Called Shiloh or One Sent....John 17:3
Genesis 49:10	To come before Judah lost identity....John 11:47-52
Genesis 49:10	To Him shall the obedience of the people be....John 10:16
Exodus 3:13,14	The Great "I Am"......John 4:26
Exodus 12:5	A Lamb without blemish....1 Peter 1:19
Exodus 12:13	The Lamb's blood saves from Roman wrath....Romans. 5:8
Exodus 12:21-27	Christ is our Passover....1 Corinthians 5:7
Exodus 12:46	Not a bone of the Lamb to be broken....John 19:31-36
Exodus 13:2	Blessing to first born son...Luke 2:23
Exodus 15:2	His exaltation predicted....Acts 7:55; 56
Exodus 15:11	His Character–Holiness....Luke 1:35; Acts 4:27
Exodus 17:6	The Spiritual Rock of Israel....1 Corinthians 10:4
Exodus 33:19	His Character–Merciful....Luke 1:72
Leviticus 14:11	Leper cleansed–Sign to priesthood...Luke 5:12-14; Acts 6:7
Leviticus 16:15-17	Prefigures Christ's once-for-all death....Hebrews 9:7-14
Leviticus 16:27	Suffering outside camp...Matthew 27:33; Hebrews 13:11, 12
Leviticus 17:11	The Blood–the life of the flesh....Matthew 26:28; Mark 10:45
Leviticus 17:11	It is the blood that makes atonement....1 John 3:14-18
Leviticus 23:37	The Drink-offering: "If any man thirst."...John 19:31-36
Numbers 9:12	Not a bone of Him broken...John 19:31-36
Numbers 21:9	The serpent on a pole–Christ lifted up....John 3:14-18
Numbers 24:8	Flight to Egypt...Matthew 2:14

Numbers 24:17	Time: "I shall see him, but not now."....Galatians 4:4	
Numbers 24:17-19	A star out of Jacob… Luke 1:33,78; Revelation 22:16	
Deuteronomy 18:15	"This is of a truth that prophet."....John 6:14	
Deuteronomy 18:16	"Had ye believed Moses, ye would believe me."....John 5:47	
Deuteronomy 18:18	Sent by the Father to speak His word....John 8:28, 29	
Deuteronomy 18:19	Whoever will not hear must bear his sin....John 12:15	
Deuteronomy 21:23	As a prophet...John 6:14; 7:40, Acts 3:22,23	
Deuteronomy 21:23	Cursed is he that hangs on a tree....Galatians 3:10-13	
Ruth 4:4-9	Christ, our kinsman, has redeemed us....Ephesians 1:3-7	
1 Samuel 2:10	Anointed King to the Lord....Matthew 28:18; John 12:15	
2 Samuel 7:12	David's Seed....Matthew 1:1	
2 Samuel 7:14a	The Son of God....Luke 1:32	
2 Samuel 7:16	David's house established forever....Luke 3:31; Rev. 22:16	
2 Samuel 23:2-4	Would be the "Rock"…1 Corinthians 10:4	
2 Samuel 23:2-4	Would be as the "light of the morning"…Revelation 22:16	
2 Kings 2:11	The bodily ascension to heaven illustrated....Luke 24:51	
1 Chronicles 17:11	David's Seed....Matthew 1:1; 9:27	
1 Chronicles 17:12	To reign on David's throne forever....Luke 1:32; 33	
1 Chronicles 17:13	I will be His Father, He....my Son."....Hebrews 1:5	
Job 19:23-27	The Resurrection predicted....John 5:24-29	
Psalms 2:1-3	The enmity of kings foreordained....Acts 4:25-28	
Psalms 2:2	To own the title, Anointed (Christ)....Acts 2:36	
Psalms 2:6	His Character–Holiness....John 8:46; Rev. 3:7	
Psalms 2:6	To own the title King....Matthew 2:2	
Psalms 2:7	Declared the Beloved Son....Matthew 3:17	
Psalms 2:7,8	The Crucifixion and Resurrection intimated....Acts 13:29-33	
Psalms 2:12	Life comes through faith in Him....John 20:31	
Psalms 8:2	The mouths of babes perfect His praise....Matthew 21:16	
Psalms 8:5, 6	Humiliation & exaltation....Luke 24:50-53; 1 Corinthians 15:27	
Psalms 16:10	Was not to see corruption....Acts 2:31	
Psalms 16:9-11	Was to arise from the dead....John 20:9	
Psalms 17:15	The resurrection predicted....Luke 24:6	
Psalms 22:1	Forsaken because of sins of others....2 Corinthians 5:21	
Psalms 22:1	Words spoken from Calvary, "My God...." Mark 15:34	
Psalms 22:2	Darkness upon Calvary....Matthew 27:45	
Psalms 22:7	They shoot out the lip and shake the head....Matthew 27:39	
Psalms 22:8	"He trusted in God, let Him deliver Him"....Matthew 27:43	
Psalms 22:9	Born the Savior....Luke 2:7	
Psalms 22:14	Died of a broken (ruptured) heart....John 19:34	
Psalms 22:14	Suffered agony on Calvary....Mark 15:34-37	
Psalms 22:15	He thirsted......John 19:28	
Psalms 22:16	They pierced His hands and His feet....John 19:34,37;20:27	
Psalms 22:17-18	Stripped Him before the stares of men....Luke 23:34,35	
Psalms 22:18	They parted His garments...John 19:23-24	

Psalms 22:20-21	He committed Himself to God....Luke 23:46
Psalms 22:20-21	Satanic power bruising the Redeemer's heel....Hebrews 2:14
Psalms 22:22	His Resurrection declared......John 20:17
Psalms 22:27	He shall be the governor of the nations....Col 1:16
Psalms 22:31	"It is finished"....John 19:30
Psalms 23:1	"I am the Good Shepherd"....John 10:11
Psalms 24:3	His exaltation predicted....Acts 1:11; Phil. 2:9
Psalms 27:12	Accused by false witnesses...Matthew 26:60,61; Mark 14:57
Psalms 30:3	His resurrection predicted....Acts 2:32
Psalms 31:5	"Into thy hands I commit my spirit"....Luke 23:46
Psalms 31:11	His acquaintances fled from Him....Mark 14:50
Psalms 31:13	They took counsel to put Him to death....John 11:53
Psalms 31:14,15	"He trusted in God, let Him deliver him"....Matthew 27:43
Psalms 34:20.	Not a bone of Him broken......John 19:31-36
Psalms 35:11	False witnesses rose up against Him....Matthew 26:59
Psalms 35:19	He was hated without a cause....John 15:25
Psalms 38:11	His friends stood afar off......Luke 23:49
Psalms 40:2-5	The joy of His resurrection predicted....John 20:20
Psalms 40:6-8	His delight–the will of the Father....John 4:34
Psalms 40:9	He was to preach the righteousness in Israel....Matthew 4:17
Psalms 40:14	Confronted by adversaries in the Garden....John
Psalms 41:9	Betrayed by a familiar friend......John 13:18
Psalms 45:2	Words of Grace come from His lips....Luke 4:22
Psalms 45:6	To own the title, God...Hebrews 1:8
Psalms 45:7	Special anointing by Holy Spirit....Matthew 3:16; Hebrews 1:9
Psalms 45:7,8	Called the Christ (Messiah or Anointed)....Luke 2:11
Psalms 49-15	His Resurrection...Acts 2:27; 13:35; Mark 16:6
Psalms 55:12-14	Betrayed by a friend, not an enemy....John 13:18
Psalms 55:15	Unrepentant death of Betrayer...Matthew 27:3-5; Acts 1:16-19
Psalms 68:18	To give gifts to men....Ephesians 4:7-16
Psalms 68:18	Ascended into Heaven....Luke 24:51
Psalms 69:4	Hated without a cause....John 15:25
Psalms 69:8	A stranger to own brethren....Luke 8:20-21
Psalms 69:9	Zealous for the Lord's House....John 2:17
Psalms 69:14-20	Anguish of soul before crucifixion...Matthew 26:36-45
Psalms 69:20	"My soul is exceeding sorrowful."....Matthew 26:38
Psalms 69:21	Given vinegar in thirst....Matthew 27:34
Psalms 69:26	The Savior given and smitten by God....John 17:4; 18:11
Psalms 72:10,11	Great persons were to visit Him....Matthew 2:1-11
Psalms 72:16	The corn of wheat to fall into the Ground....John 12:24
Psalms 72:17	His name will produce offspring....John 1:12,13
Psalms 72:17	All nations shall be blessed by Him....Acts 2:11-12,41
Psalms 78:1.2	He would teach in parables....Matthew 13:34-35
Psalms 78:2b	To speak the Wisdom of God with authority....Matthew 7:29

APPENDIX 189

Psalms 88:8	They stood afar off and watched....Luke 23:49	
Psalms 89:26	Messiah will call God His Father....Matthew 11:27	
Psalms 89:27	Emmanuel to be higher than earthly kings....Luke 1:32-33	
Psalms 89:35-37	David's Seed, throne, kingdom endure forever....Luke 1:32-33	
Psalms 89:36-37	His character–Faithfulness....Rev. 1:5	
Psalms 90:2	He is from everlasting (Micah 5:2)....John 1:1	
Psalms 91:11-12	Identified as Messianic; used to tempt Christ....Luke 4:10-11	
Psalms 97:9	His exaltation predicted....Acts 1:11; Ephesians 1:20	
Psalms 100:5	His character–Goodness....Matthew 19:16,17	
Psalms 102:1-11	The Suffering and Reproach of Calvary....John 21:16-30	
Psalms 102:16	Son of Man comes in Glory...Luke 21:24; Revelation 12:5-10	
Psalms 102:25-27	Messiah is the Preexistent Son....Hebrews 1:10-12	
Psalms 109:4	Prayed for His enemies...Luke 23:34	
Psalms 109:7-8	Another to succeed Judas...Acts 1:16-20	
Psalms 109:25	Ridiculed....Matthew 27:39	
Psalms 110:1	Son of David....Matthew 22:43	
Psalms 110:1	To ascend to the right-hand of the Father....Mark 16:19	
Psalms 110:1	David's son called Lord....Matthew 22:44-45	
Psalms 110:4	A priest after Melchizedek's order....Hebrews 6:20	
Psalms 112:4	His character-compassionate, gracious, etc.... Matthew 9:36	
Psalms 118:17-18	His resurrection assured....Luke 24:5-7; 1 Corinthians 15:20	
Psalms 118:22-23	The rejected stone is Head of the corner....Matthew 21:42-43	
Psalms 118:26a	The Blessed One presented to Israel....Matthew 21:9	
Psalms 118:26b	To come while Temple standing....Matthew 21:12-15	
Psalms 132:11	Seed of David (the fruit of His Body)....Luke 1:32	
Psalms 138:1-6	Supremacy of David's Seed amazes kings....Matthew 2:2-6	
Psalms 147:3,6	The earthly ministry of Christ described....Luke 4:18	
Psalms 1:23	He will send the Spirit of God....John 16:7	
Proverbs 8:22-23	The Messiah would be from everlasting...John 17:5	
Proverbs 30:4	Declared the Son of God...John 3:13, Romans 1:2-4; 10:6-9	
Song of Sol. 5:16	The altogether lovely One....John 1:17	
Isaiah 2:2-4	Repentance for the nations...Luke 24:47	
Isaiah 5:1-6	Son of God's vineyard: a parable of judgment	
Isaiah 6:1	When Isaiah saw His glory....John 12:40-41	
Isaiah 6:9-10	Parables fall on deaf ears....Matthew 13:13-15	
Isaiah 6:9-12	Blinded to Christ and deaf to His words....Acts 28:23-29	
Isaiah 7:14	To be born of a virgin....Luke 1:35	
Isaiah 7:14	To be Emmanuel–God with us....Matthew 1:18-23	
Isaiah 8:8	Called Emmanuel....Matthew 28:20	
Isaiah 8:14	A stone of stumbling, a Rock of offense....1 Pet. 2:8	
Isaiah 9:1-2	His ministry to begin in Galilee....Matthew 4:12-17	
Isaiah 9:6	A child born–Humanity....Luke 1:31	
Isaiah 9:6	A Son given–Deity....Luke 1:32; John 1:14; 1 Tim. 3:16	
Isaiah 9:6	Declared to be the Son of God with power....Romans 1:3-4	

Isaiah 9:6	The Wonderful One....Luke 4:22
Isaiah 9:6	The Counselor....Matthew 13:54
Isaiah 9:6	The Mighty God....Matthew 11:20
Isaiah 9:6	The Everlasting Father....John 8:58
Isaiah 9:6	The Prince of Peace...John 16:33; Ephesians 2:14
Isaiah 9:7	To establish an everlasting kingdom....Luke 1:32-33
Isaiah 9:7	His Character—Just....John 5:30
Isaiah 9:7	No end to his government, throne, and peace....Luke 1:32-33
Isaiah 11:1	Called a Nazarene–the Branch....Matthew 2:23
Isaiah 11:1	A rod out of Jesse–Son of Jesse....Luke 3:23,32
Isaiah 11:2	The anointed One by the Spirit....Matthew 3:16-17
Isaiah 11:2	His Character–Wisdom, Understanding, et al....John 4:4-26
Isaiah 11:4	His Character–Truth....John 14:6
Isaiah 11:10	The Gentiles seek Him....John 12:18-21
Isaiah 12:2	Called Jesus–Yeshua (salvation)....Matthew 1:21
Isaiah 16:4-5	Reigning in mercy...Luke 1:31-33
Isaiah 22:21-25	Peg in a sure place...Revelation 3:7
Isaiah 25:8	Victory over death....1 Corinthians 15:54
Isaiah 26:19	His power of Resurrection predicted....John 11:43-44
Isaiah 28:16	The Messiah is the precious corner stone....Acts 4:11-12
Isaiah 29:13	Indicated hypocritical obedience to His Word....Matthew 15:7-9
Isaiah 29:14	Wise are confounded by the Word....1 Corinthians 1:18-31
Isaiah 32:2	A Refuge–A man shall be a hiding place....Matthew 23:37
Isaiah 33:22	Son of the Highest...Luke 1:32; 1 Timothy 1:17 6:15
Isaiah 35:4	He will come and save you....Matthew 1:21
Isaiah 35:5	To have a ministry of miracles....Matthew 11:4-6
Isaiah 40:3-4	Preceded by forerunner....John 1:23
Isaiah 40:9	"Behold your God."....John 1:36;19:14
Isaiah 40:11	A shepherd–compassionate life-giver....John 10:10-18
Isaiah 42:1-4	A servant–a faithful, patient redeemer....Matthew 12:18-21
Isaiah 42:2	Meek and lowly....Matthew 11:28-30
Isaiah 42:3	He brings hope for the hopeless....John 4
Isaiah 42:4	The nations shall wait on His teachings....John 12:20-26
Isaiah 42:6	The Light (salvation) of the Gentiles....Luke 2:32
Isaiah 42:1,6	His has worldwide compassion....Matthew 28:19-20
Isaiah 42:7.	Blind eyes opened....John 9:25-38
Isaiah 42:13-25	Messiah's actions at His second coming...Revelation
Isaiah 43:11	He is the only Savior....Acts 4:12
Isaiah 44:3	He will send the Spirit of God....John 16:7,13
Isaiah 45:23	He will be the Judge....John 5:22; Romans 14:11
Isaiah 48:12	The First and the Last....John 1:30; Revelation 1:8,17
Isaiah 48:17	He came as a Teacher....John 3:2
Isaiah 49:1	Called from the womb–His humanity....Matthew 1:18
Isaiah 49:5	A Servant from the womb....Luke 1:31; Philippians 2:7

APPENDIX 191

Isaiah 49:6	He is Salvation for Israel....Luke 2:29-32
Isaiah 49:6	He is the Light of the Gentiles....Acts 13:47
Isaiah 49:6	He is Salvation unto the ends of the earth....Acts 15:7-18
Isaiah 49:7	He is despised of the Nation....John 8:48-49
Isaiah 50:3	Sky is clothed in black at His humiliation....Luke 23:44-45
Isaiah 50:4	He is a learned counselor for the weary....Matthew 11:28-29
Isaiah 50:5.	The Servant bound willingly to obedience....Matthew 26:39
Isaiah 50:6a	"I gave my back to the smiters."....Matthew 27:26
Isaiah 50:6b	He was smitten on the cheeks....Matthew 26:67
Isaiah 50:6c	He was spat upon....Matthew 27:30
Isaiah 52:4-5	Suffered vicariously...Mark 15:3-4,27-28; Luke 23:1-25,32-34
Isaiah 52:7	To publish good tidings of peace....Luke 4:14-15
Isaiah 52:13	The Servant exalted....Acts 1:8-11; Ephesians 1:19-22
Isaiah 52:13	Behold, My Servant....Matthew 17:5; Phil. 2:5-8
Isaiah 52:14	Shockingly abused....Luke 18:31-34; Matthew 26:67-68
Isaiah 52:15	Nations startled by His message...Romans. 15:18-21
Isaiah 52:15	His blood shed to make atonement for all....Rev. 1:5
Isaiah 53:1	His people would not believe Him....John 12:37-38
Isaiah 53:2a	He would grow up in a poor family....Luke 2:7
Isaiah 53:2b	Appearance of an ordinary man....Phil. 2:7-8
Isaiah 53:3a	Despised....Luke 4:28-29
Isaiah 53:3b	Rejected....Matthew 27:21-23
Isaiah 53:3	Great sorrow and grief....Luke 19:41-42
Isaiah 53:3d	Men hide from being associated with Him....Mark 14:50-52
Isaiah 53:4a	He would have a healing ministry....Luke 6:17-19
Isaiah 53:4b	He would bear the sins of the world....1 Pet. 2:24
Isaiah 53:4c	Thought to be cursed by God....Matthew 27:41-43
Isaiah 53:5a	Bears penalty for mankind's transgressions....Luke 23:33
Isaiah 53:5b	His sacrifice provided peace between man and God....Col. 1:20
Isaiah 53:5c	His back would be whipped....Matthew 27:26
Isaiah 53:6a	He would be the sin-bearer for all mankind....Galatians 1:4
Isaiah 53:6b	God's will that He bear sin for all mankind....1 John 4:10
Isaiah 53:7a	Oppressed and afflicted....Matthew 27:27-31
Isaiah 53:7b	Silent before his accusers....Matthew 27:12-14
Isaiah 53:7c	Sacrificial lamb....John 1:29
Isaiah 53:8a	Confined and persecuted....Matthew 26:47-27:31
Isaiah 53:8b	He would be judged....John 18:13-22
Isaiah 53:8c	Killed....Matthew 27:35
Isaiah 53:8d	Died for the sins of the world....1 John 2:2
Isaiah 53:9a	Buried in a rich man's grave....Matthew 27:57
Isaiah 53:9b	Innocent and had done no violence....Mark 15:3
Isaiah 53:9c	No deceit in his mouth....John 18:38
Isaiah 53:10a	God's will that He die for mankind....John 18:11
Isaiah 53:10b	An offering for sin....Matthew 20:28

Isaiah 53:10c	Resurrected and live forever....Mark 16:16
Isaiah 53:10d	He would prosper....John 17:1-5
Isaiah 53:11a	God fully satisfied with His suffering....John 12:27
Isaiah 53:11b	God's servant....Romans. 5:18-19
Isaiah 53:11c	He would justify man before God....Romans. 5:8-9
Isaiah 53:11d	The sin-bearer for all mankind....Hebrews 9:28
Isaiah 53:12a	Exalted by God because of his sacrifice....Matthew 28:18
Isaiah 53:12b	He would give up his life to save mankind....Luke 23:46
Isaiah 53:12c	Grouped with criminals....Luke 23:32
Isaiah 53:12d	Sin-bearer for all mankind....2 Corinthians 5:21
Isaiah 53:12e	Interceded to God in behalf of mankind....Luke 23:34
Isaiah 55:1	Every one come who is thirsty...New Testament
Isaiah 55:3	Resurrected by God....Acts 13:34
Isaiah 55:4	A witness....John 18:37
Isaiah 55:5	Foreign nations come to God...Acts
Isaiah 59:15-16a	He would come to provide salvation....John 6:40
Isaiah 59:15-16b	Intercessor between man and God....Matthew 10:32
Isaiah 59:20	He would come to Zion as their Redeemer....Luke 2:38
Isaiah 60:1-3	Nations walk in the light...Luke 2:32
Isaiah 61:1a	The Spirit of God upon him....Matthew 3:16-17
Isaiah 61:1b	The Messiah would preach the good news....Luke 4:17-21
Isaiah 61:1c	Provided freedom from bondage of sin and death....John 8:32
Isaiah 61:1-2	Would provide freedom from condemnation....John 5:24
Isaiah 62:1-2	Called by a new name...Luke 2:32, Revelation 3:12
Isaiah 62:10-12	Would enter Jerusalem...Matthew 21:7
Isaiah 63:1-3	A vesture dipped in blood...Revelation 19:13
Isaiah 63:8-9	Afflicted with the afflicted...Matthew 25:34-40
Isaiah 65:9	Seed out of Jacob...Hebrews 7:14; Revelation 5:5
Isaiah 65:17-25	New heaven/New Earth...2 Peter 3:13, Revelation 21:1
Isaiah 66:18-19	All nations come to God...New Testament
Jeremiah 23:5-6a	Descendant of David....Luke 3:23-31
Jeremiah 23:5-6b	The Messiah would be God....John 13:13
Jeremiah 23:5-6c	The Messiah would be both God and Man....1 Tim. 3:16
Jeremiah 30:9	Born a King...John 18:37, Revelation 1:5
Jeremiah 31:15	Massacre of infants...Matthew 2:16-18
Jeremiah 31:22	Born of a virgin....Matthew 1:18-20
Jeremiah 31:31	The Messiah would be the new covenant....Matthew 26:28
Jeremiah 33:14-15	Descendant of David....Luke 3:23-31
Ezekiel 17:22-24	Descendant of David....Luke 3:23-31
Ezekiel 21:26-27	The humble exalted...Luke 1:52
Ezekiel 34:23-24	Descendant of David....Matthew 1:1
Daniel 2:34-35	Stone cut without hands....Acts 4:10-12
Daniel 2:44-45	His Kingdom triumphant....Luke 1:33; Revelation 11:15
Dan. 7:13-14a	He would ascend into heaven....Acts 1:9-11

APPENDIX 193

Dan. 7:13-14b	Highly exalted....Ephesians 1:20-22	
Dan. 7:13-14c	His dominion would be everlasting....Luke 1:31-33	
Daniel 7:27	Kingdom for the Saints....Luke 1:33; Revelation 11:15	
Dan. 9:24a	To make an end to sins....Galatians 1:3-5	
Dan. 9:24b	He would be holy....Luke 1:35	
Dan. 9:25	Announced to his people 483 years, to the exact day, after the decree to rebuild the city of Jerusalem....John 12:12-13	
Dan. 9:26a	Killed....Matthew 27:35	
Dan. 9:26b	Died for the sins of the world....Hebrews 2:9	
Dan. 9:26c	Killed before destruction of the temple....Matthew 27:50-51	
Dan. 10:5-6	Messiah in a glorified state....Rev. 1:13-16	
Hosea 3:5	Israel restored....John 18:37, Romans 11:25-27	
Hosea 11:1	Flight to Egypt....Matthew 2:14	
Hosea 13:14	He would defeat death....1 Corinthians 15:55-57	
Joel 2:28-32	Promise of the Spirit....Acts 2:17-21, Romans 10:13	
Joel 2:32	Offer salvation to all mankind....Romans 10:12-13	
Micah 2:12-13	Israel regathered....John 10:14,26	
Micah 4:1-8	The Kingdom established....Luke 1:33, Matthew 2:1,	
Micah 5:2a	Born in Bethlehem....Matthew 2:1-2	
Micah 5:2b	God's servant....John 15:10	
Micah 5:2c	From everlasting....John 8:58	
Haggai 2:6-9	Visited the second Temple....Luke 2:27-32	
Haggai 2:23	Descendant of Zerubbabel....Luke 3:23-27	
Joel 2:28-32	Promise of the Spirit....Acts 2:17-21, Romans 10:13	
Amos 8:9	The Sun Darkened....Matthew 24:29, Acts 2:20	
Amos 9:11-12	Restoration of tabernacle....Acts 14:16-18	
Habakkuk 2:14	Earth filled with knowledge of Lord's glory....Romans 11:26	
Zechariah 2:10-13	The Lamb on the Throne....Revelation 5:13, 6:9, 21:24	
Zechariah 3:8	God's servant....John 17:4	
Zechariah 6:12-13	Priest and King....Hebrews 8:1	
Zechariah 9:9a	Greeted with rejoicing in Jerusalem....Matthew 21:8-10	
Zechariah 9:9b	Beheld as King....John 12:12-13	
Zechariah 9:9c	The Messiah would be just....John 5:30	
Zechariah 9:9d	The Messiah would bring salvation....Luke 19:10	
Zechariah 9:9e	The Messiah would be humble....Matthew 11:29	
Zechariah 9:9f	Presented to Jerusalem riding on a donkey....Matthew 21:6-9	
Zechariah 10:4	The cornerstone....Ephesians 2:20	
Zechariah 11:4-6a	At His coming, Israel to have unfit leaders....Matthew 23:1-4	
Zechariah 11:4-6b	Rejection causes God to remove protection...Luke 19:41-44	
Zechariah 11:4-6c	Rejected in favor of another king....John 19:13-15	
Zechariah 11:7	Ministry to "poor," the believing remnant... Matthew 9:35-36	
Zechariah 11:8a	Unbelief forces Messiah to reject them....Matthew 23:33	
Zechariah 11:8b	Despised....Matthew 27:20	
Zechariah 11:9	Spoke in parables....Matthew 13:10-11	

Zechariah 11:10-11	Rejection causes God to remove protection....Luke 19:41-44
Zechariah 11:10-11	The Messiah would be God....John 14:7
Zechariah 11:12-13	Betrayed for thirty pieces of silver....Matthew 26:14-15
Zechariah 11:12-13	Rejected....Matthew 26:14-15
Zechariah 11:12-13	Thirty pieces of silver cast into Lord's house...Matthew 27:3-5
Zechariah 11:12-13	The Messiah would be God....John 12:45
Zechariah 12:10a	The Messiah's body would be pierced....John 19:34-37
Zechariah 12:10b	The Messiah would be both God and man....John 10:30
Zechariah 12:10c	The Messiah would be rejected....John 1:11
Zechariah 13:7a	God's will He die for mankind....John 18:11
Zechariah 13:7b	A violent death....Matthew 27:35
Zechariah 13:7c	Both God and man....John 14:9
Zechariah 13:7d	Israel scattered as result of rejecting Him...Matthew 26:31-56
Malachi 3:1a	Messenger to prepare the way for Messiah....Matthew 11:10
Malachi 3:1b	Sudden appearance at the temple....Mark 11:15-16
Malachi 3:1c	Messenger of the new covenant....Luke 4:43
Malachi 3:3	Our Sins Are Purged...Luke 1:78, John 1:9; 12:46, 2 Peter 1:19
Malachi 4:5	Forerunner in the spirit of Elijah...Matthew 3:1-2
Malachi 4:6	Forerunner would turn many to righteousness....Luke 1:16-17

List adapted from the following sources:
http://www.bibleprobe.com/365messianicprophecies.htm
http://www.hopeofisrael.net
http://www.historicbelt.com/pb-family/proph.html
http://www.messiahrevealed.org/

SUGGESTED ANSWERS:

CHAPTER 1
THE LIMITS OF PROOF:
1. Nature as observed intelligently.
2. People accumulate knowledge over time. Time is a process revealing things progressively and increasing accountability.
3. It is readily observable by our senses and comprehensible by our conscience.
4. The order and precision of natural laws and particles gives stern witness for unrivaled competence conceiving it and sustaining it.
5. Many answers could be suggested (e.g. Fingerprints of a suspect match those found at a crime scene).
6. The atoms are too many, too small, and too fast to ever get a comprehensive result. Only a generalized answer based on specific samples is possible.
7. If God cannot do enough to evidence His own existence, He is not much of a God. Anyone who feels an obligation to prove that God merely exists, has a weak concept of God and shows a disregard for the obvious.
8. It depends upon the objective honesty of those in the discussion. Investigative discussions can be carried on indefinitely, unless those involved are objectively honest or an authority intervenes.
9. They do not like the truth it implies.
10. Pride. A desire to defend one's own judgements and an unwillingness to respect the judgements of another.
11. Everyone would be blind and without eyes. Also as a result, the population would likely be far less because of the life-threatening hazards associated with blindness.
12. Adam and Eve.
13. The universe's "gradual unfolding toward higher disorder." (Entropy.)
14. Rampant doubt.
15. Insufficient evidence.
16. The use of a timeframe that spans billions of years assumes that there will never be direct substantial evidence.

THE EXPECTATIONS FOR PROOF ANSWERS:
1. A substantial minimum of evidence.
2. Both can be confirmed by the fulfillment of their predictions. They can both be invalidated, if their predictions fail to be fulfilled.
3. No.
4. May 14, 1948.
5. Death penalty.
6. A "finely graduated organic chain."
7. A missing fossil chain.
8. The sudden introduction in earth's fossil record of all the major species groups.
9. Abrupt Creation and global floods.
10. A biologist and key contributor to the modern synthesis of evolutionary theory.
11. All the world's species groups were soft-bodied before, and then all the fossilized species that can now be observed there grew skeletons around or inside existing bodies in a practically synchronized fashion.
12. Some other areas of study that show this are 1)the development of variation, 2)genetic heritage, 3)radiocarbon dating, 4)minimum complexity, and 5)the practical *utility* of natural selection.
13. Natural mutations will consistently create variation to provide options for natural selection to work with.
14. 500 or more.
15. Coelacanth (pronounced "seel-uh-canth").
16. 2,000 to 4,000 times the age of East Africa's Lake Victoria.
17. Blue-green algae.
18. Its "morphological stasis" (that it still looks the same).
19. It must occur only in defined cycles.
20. We expect the Author of life to make things that hold up well in consistency with His eternal nature.
21. Progress
22. It makes no attempt at explaining the origin of life.
23. That consequences define right and wrong.
24. In some other unknown *universe*.

THE CONCLUSIONS WITH PROOF ANSWERS:
1. To get a conclusion.
2. Conclusions that spring forcibly from our concentrated sense of truth.
3. Many answers could be suggested (e.g. a sturdy looking chair is safe to sit on).
4. Because someone who doubts everything cannot know anything, and therefore cannot be wise.
5. Life originating from lifeless objects (only cells make cells).
6. The first law of thermodynamics (conservation of energy).
7. Mass and life were supernaturally created.
8. The first cause is a divine <u>Person</u>.
9. Many answers chould be suggested (e.g. Galileo Galilei, Isaac Newton, William Paley, George Washington Carver, James Clerk Maxwell, Michael Faraday, Lord Kelvin, Albert Einstein, Francis Collins [current]).
10. A cell.
11. Yes.
12. The biologist Carolus Linnaeus.
13. It appears that his imagined tree of descent or the like never existed literally.
14. Because the truth about real-world events must ultimately be <u>felt</u>.
15. The physical properties of light.
16. Invariance theory.
17. Time for that person is stretched (dilated) [relative to the speed of light, so that the speed of light never changes from any perspective].
18. We are all moving at roughly the same velocity. [The rotation of our galaxy and earth's orbit and rotation make other motion practically negligible.]
19. Yes (and the event also eternally occupies its point in spacetime).

CHAPTER 2
THE TAPROOT OF IRRESPONSIBILITY:
1. Many answers could be suggested
   (e.g. A well-educated criminal is a more destructive criminal).
2. All hope for another (tolerated) person behaving properly is gone.
3. Real love will try to help the situation rather than ignoring it.
4. Yes.
5. The Old Deluder Satan Act (a.k.a. Massachusetts General School Law of 1647).
6. Spiritual literacy by well-facilitated study of Christian Scripture.
7. They refuse to accept that their true need is an inner spiritual one.
8. The life and ministry of the Man Jesus Christ.
9. He distained it.
10. If he was openly averse to spiritual responsibility, it would be irrational to expect personal integrity in matters of his scientific analysis.
11. Self-deception to avoid a sense of vulnerability (…"I did no wrong").
12. An extreme case of self-deception to avoid guilt.
13. "I could not imagine being an atheist at any time before 1859, when Darwin's *Origin of Species* was published."
14. Yes (because without responsibility evil cannot be identified, and so it cannot be defended against).
15. Anxiety and fear.
16. It is a useful resource to establish character (While this is common sense, it is also verified by modern science).
17. a) They struggle to identify harmful vices in a second generation.
    b) The sense of authority that he or she ought to maintain is impaired.
18. To avoid responsibility for them.
19. It assumes that all the vast wealth of nature is cheap and easy.
20. "freely"
21. Many answers could be suggested
(e.g. No basis for personal responsibility… Depression due to bad "fate").
22. Free will.

REVIEW ANSWERS 199

THE TAPROOT OF NEGLIGENCE:
1. Ingratitude.
2. Neglect and ignorance of the Bible's content.
3. The Roman Catholic Church.
4. Spiritual darkness.
5. It provides objects to think about.
6. Isaiah 40:22.
7. Christopher Columbus.
8. Psalm 19:4.
9. They believe that human intellect is the final Word of life.
10. They have been religious tyrants.
11. Darwinism is not valid science for American public classrooms.
12. Playing naïve about the real and devastating consequences of evil. "Rose-colored glasses" (other good answers can be suggested).
13 Yes (see Romans 8:22).
14. It is a reminder of sin's consequences (see Genesis 3:14–19).
15. Many answers could be suggested (e.g. they restrict us, simplifying and stabilizing life).
16. Sam Harris (a secular psychologist and neuroscientist).
17. The human heart tends to be very deceitful (other good answers may be suggested).
18. Yes (Harris thinks it will someday be created... Bible students, in contrast, have found that it already exists and is quite accessible).

THE TAPROOT OF DISRESPECT:
1. [re-] "back" + [spect] "look at"... It carries the idea of "look back at." (And so <u>dis</u>respect will tend to overlook important things).
2. So that the brain receives all the information from the left and right bundled respectively.
3. Larger than North America.
4. Because the goal of humanism is to elevate the human intellect and show how it is superior to all things beside it.
5. Yes (biologist Massimo Pigliucci among others).
6. "a single cell in the body of its author"
7. Less than 10^{99} (see chapter 2 endnote #39 [3.2×10^{96} events]).

8. Writing Encyclopedia Britannica randomly or the far more complex unassisted origin of life. (With our highly advanced technology it would be extremely difficult or even impossible to design and build any viable living cell from available raw materials. Which means it is likely far more complicated than designing and building a cutting-edge Macintosh computer).
9. Heroes provide an object to emulate and, in that way, they provide useful direction and promote personal achievements.
10. "Holy" (He is the complete and final standard for proper conduct).
11. Divine holiness (as revealed in the Scripture).
12. By human logic (rationalizing).
13. Such an approach would waste the wisdom of our conscience and would lead to treacherous spiritual disorientation as a result.
14. Many answers could be suggested
(e.g. They gain our attention so that we can see more important matters).
15. He lacks respect for the nature of God as revealed in Scripture. (Harris envisions an impulsive tyrant, because he has no true concept of God.)
16. The eternal holy nature of the immutable God (see Hebrews 13:8 and Colossians 1:17).
17. No answer (trick question).
18. It causes evolution to trend toward disorder.
19. Neutral.
20. They have not had any bona fide improvement since the spontaneous beginning of first life (They are not very impressive).

THE TAPROOT OF SELFISHNESS:
1. An attitude of living ultimately for self.
2. Yes.
3. Many answers could be suggested (e.g. As people mature they should realize that they are a very small part of a more important reality).
4. "Survival of the fittest."
5. Nature has no need of multicellular organisms and will not finance the project of bringing individual cells together.

6. Trusted scientists within mainstream secular science.
7. Humans generally have a deep-seated appreciation for selflessness (though we tend to fail at living out selflessness).
8. Jesus Christ.
9. Humans are made in the image of God and can sense that genuine giving is godly, and that God always outgives them (see Romans 5:8; Acts 20:35).
10. Ulterior motives (Acting kind for selfish reasons).
11. Many answers could be suggested (e.g. Paul [see Philippians 3:8; Romans 9:1–3] and John the Baptist [see John 3:30]).
12. Many answers could be suggested (e.g. Be advised that the world is watching them and search their motives to please God above all. As the Apostle Paul "die daily" [see 1Corinthians 15:31; Colossians 3:1-11]).
13. Deny.
14. Yes.

THE TAPROOT OF PRIDE:
1. The oldest portions of Scripture (Old Testament) were to be disregarded as well as many other passages.
2. An act of taking brazen liberties with or running off with another person's assets—especially assets that are entrusted to us.
3. Reality.
4. "Humus" (meaning "earth"—carrying the idea of soil).
5. Erik Erikson
6. Many answers could be suggested (e.g. God never has an identity crisis and He will be much more reliable than us through life's challenges).
7. The word "pride" is introduced with the prepositional phrase "of your power" hinting that an emphasis on human capabilities feeds empty pride.
8. Human (Aryan) intellect and capabilities.
9. They must be personally grounded in humility (They must be willing to accept God's Word as final and not attempt to challenge or redefine it).
10. The complex stories forming Darwinism sound more sophisticated and cater to their pride much better than simple creation accounts.

11. Ideas that pass stealthily from generation to generation. (He thinks that the human sense of God and truth are "memes").
12. The telephone game.
13. Because the final truth most essential to life itself is often discredited carelessly by the very people entrusted by many for its accuracy.
14. It was produced in faith and prayer using what God had sovereignly preserved. (All modern versions, in contrast, are attempts to <u>reconstruct</u> a lost book—generally with an unabashed leaning toward intellectualism. In short, the King James Bible is based on faith rather than doubt). Also, the textual resources and linguistic skill of translators were, in fact, superior.
15. They trust that modern methods of textual criticism are successfully restructuring what has been poorly kept (by God) over the years.
16. Yes.
17. He has appealed to their ego claiming his doctrine is reason-based (Pride then provides an invitation for deception [see Obadiah 1:3]).
18. Secular evolution versus creation.
19. We will find our minds more gifted.
20. We are prone to slip deeper and deeper into pretenses and after a while lose touch altogether with real sincere humility.
21. Unlike science, the Word of God is final and clear NOT tentative.

CHAPTER 3
THE FAITH FOR COGNITION:
1. Phantasms.
2. It takes time for light to travel to us, and it takes time for us to process nerve impulses.
3. The concept of a distinct present (now) does not and apparently <u>can</u> not have a place in physics.
4. In many areas we have to imply the information that is not available based on the information that is available; faith is the wisdom to do so.
5. It means "turned into one" (It is a testimony to the unified character of nature).
6. Energy.
7. A quantum.

8. The universe is connected somehow (There's no clear scientific answer yet [see Colossians 1:17 for a Bible answer]).
9. A schema.
10. When that person feels a broad category of schemas is trustworthy.
11. They have no resources to progress mentally.
12. Someone else (even a trust in natural law assumes that someone or something is maintaining the consistency of those laws).
13. They cannot appreciate the gifts sustaining them, since recognizing the gifts would be admitting that their control is contingent on the gifts.
14. They are stark reminders that human nature includes some very serious spiritual problems that we each need to confront introspectively and aggressively.
15. Because human nature is not otherwise honest enough to allow it (He is the Spirit of truth that will guide us into all truth [see John 16:13]).

THE FAITH FOR VISION:
1. Gravity or true faith can be defined as a substantial, invisible property of a nearby object.
2. It reveals things to us that would be otherwise obscure.
3. It reveals evidence of a nearby object that has gone unnoticed.
4. No (Everybody must pursue something that they believe in or they will never make any real progress [see Proverbs 29:18]).
5. Creative/insightful mind (to visualize an assortment of future events).
6. Elimination
7. In Darwinistic terms they can be nothing but lucky genetic accidents. The Bible explanation is that they were intelligently designed and formed.
8. It would tend to reduce complexity.
9. An Austrian monk named Gregor Mendel (he bred and observed pea plants on the property of a monastery).
10. Recessive genetic traits can be unseen for a while, but at times become flesh. Godly faith is true information about unseen physical events.
11. A Punnett square.

12. Both of its pod-color genes are recessive (green-forming).
13. It can only use the traits that already exist.
14. $(2)^7=128$ combinations.
15. A lack of planned order (and thus that nature was not of God).
16. Because Darwin, like many in his time, knew nothing about genetics; and so major variation in a species seemed like an ungodly lack of order.
17. The available traits being selected for are all expressed.
18. Often as much as 7 times the age.
19. They are traumatized; they are humiliated—their god dies.
20. Atheists.
21. They have no central purpose for living.
22. It once meant a point of navigation (North Star) but now means a chief inspiration.
23. They are motivated beyond natural limits of compassion by the Holy Spirit.
24. They serve as clutter, to confuse issues that should be distinct.

THE FAITH FOR EDUCABILITY:
1. Fear of water
2. Education leads students from the known to the unknown; and it is only possible to know a thing by faith, thus without faith education has no basis.
3. Many answers could be suggested
   (e.g. The desire to help in real-life situations can grow weak).
4. Over 2½ hours.
5. It can become difficult to believe anything... (ultimately resulting in a loss of interest in life).
6. Trust (faith/belief).
7. The heart (the rationalizing human nature).
8. Harris did not understand divine reasoning because it must be taught by the Holy Spirit. Harris was not willing to listen to final truth.
9. Impressively stable, existing genetic information.
10. "Recombination in a population" (existing genes are reshuffled).
11. The set of natural prime numbers (2, 3, 5, 7, 11, 13, 17...).

12. A number of genes that work together to produce varying degrees of a given trait like skin color (allowing a spectrum of options for a trait).
13. Because every cell has a full copy of the whole body's genetic information; yet a body is a diverse structure, requiring distinct cell types.
14. Genes represent a library of hidden information that is gradually revealed; true faith provides a wealth of instructive insights that are gradually revealed as true physically.

CHAPTER 4:
THE WEIGHT OF APPEARANCES:
1. Observation.
2. Many answers could be suggested (e.g. Repeatable [symmetric] natural events imply and confirm scientific laws).
3. Symmetry.
4. "absurd in the highest possible degree."
5. A password.
6. No (The author's mother is a great example of how little it affects).
7. The constancy of Almighty God.
8. Designed.
9. The second law.
10. An amplified degree of natural disorder.
11. The Higgs field (A general explanation of existing power).
12. Because he felt that the presence of God was throughout nature.
13. Colossians 1:17.
14. They "assume both design and intention behind natural events."

THE PLASTICITY OF APPEARANCES:
1. William Chaloner
2. That the appearance of developing embryos illustrates their Darwinistic descent from simpler life forms.
3. "Ontogeny recapitulates phylogeny."
4. They are the "academic equivalent of murder."

5. Henry Gee, the Chief Science Writer for *Nature*.
6. Existing genes will produce abundant variation in a population and similar individuals in that population will tend to be attracted to one another and to similar niches (polarizing distinct races and subspecies and doing precisely what is stressed in the early chapters of the book of Genesis—biological reproduction inherently tending toward distinct kinds).
7. They are all still cichlid fish (there was no phyletic evolution).
8. Because they do not make sense genetically and thus could have never existed literally.
9. Because none of the unusual species that they emphasize realistically imply an intermediate. It's like finding a fossilized apple and celebrating "the ancestor of the modern orange." (e.g. Archaeopteryx).
10. No (Long before Charles Darwin, Carolus Linnaeus categorized body structures
11. Because living ape species have body structure somewhat similar to human body structure, and extinct ape species are no closer in structure.
12. The genes of apes are in a quite different structure, and cannot all even be compared one-on-one per location to the genes of humans.
13. Extinct apes that Darwinists use to discuss a failed theory of human origins (They habitually fail to support Darwinism).
14. The principle that scenarios involving less unrelated similarities are more believable (An attempt to minimize unrelated biological parallels).
15. Because the life forms that Darwinists assume to be physically related, do not appear to be related at a genetic or molecular level.
16. Darwinism
17. "a change in the frequencies of the genes found in natural populations."
18. They see an unfamiliar trait and assume that is the result of a recent mutation; when, in fact, a majority of unfamiliar traits are simply recessive.
19. They believed in a literal descent of man from apes and were not well versed with principles of genetic heritage and recessive traits.
20. There were a few resident bacteria resistant to antibiotics and they became the majority when other bacteria were thinned out.

REVIEW ANSWERS   207

21. The genes of a normal fruit fly restrain a second set of wings to produce halters that aid in flight. When mutations destroyed the genetic restraints used in halter development, the second set of wings grew out.
22. Either intelligent forces or pre-existing biological structures.
23. A reduction of influence is not equivalent to a reduction of presence (e.g. a flat tire limits a motorist's options but does not limit his presence).
24. Common, everyday scenarios that teach eternal truth.

CHAPTER 5

THE JURISDICTION OF THE SETTING:
1. He was in the low-friction, low-gravity environment of the moon's surface (he was not bound by earthly limits).
2. Realistic concepts will agree with the local laws and conditions.
3. "No weapon that is formed against thee shall prosper; and every tongue that shall rise against thee in judgment thou shalt condemn."
4. He believes it's all about genes and external factors.
5. It will take very close to 5,730 years (the half-life of carbon 14).
6. It would take three half-lives ($1/2^3=1/8$) 3 x 5,730 years=17,190 years.
7. The point at which the C14 being produced on earth in one day by solar radiation balances the amount of earth's C14 that decays in one day.
8. Less than 30,000 years.
9. That earth used to be more radioactively clean, and that the process leading to dynamic equilibrium was still taking place very recently (strongly indicating that the earth is less than 30,000 years old).
10. The timeframes provided by carbon dating represent the half-lives of C14, and assessing half of an unknown ratio will always be inconclusive.
11. Survival of the fittest, specifically where death by predators eliminates all those who lack superior traits.

12. Because biological complexity consists of immensely precise details that would need to be selected for individually (it's the only scenario that makes sense mathematically).
13. Because the mutations that geneticists can observe are harmful.
14. They are not different theoretically, because they are just as unlikely to result in anything beneficial (they would just burn more time). Tiny accumulating mutations will actually tend to destroy genes altogether.
15. Many answers could be suggested (e.g. death stops all brain activity and shows limits of the human mind).
16. Because God made the laws, and He is outside of them; whereas the natural sciences are nothing more than a study of His natural laws.
17. a) He says that people like some control, but free will is an illusion.
    b) He says people like good friends, but selfishness drives everything.
18. Spiritual healing.

THE IMPLICATION OF THE SETTING:
1. Biologist Ernst Mayr, a secular evolutionist.
2. Psalm 9:16b "the wicked is snared in the work of his own hands." Many other passages can be suggested.
3. Parables.
4. Because sexual reproduction is widely observed throughout nature, and it is common knowledge that we exist by means of it.
5. Because truth is unaffected by arguments and opinions. Natural revelations expose fixed realities that are undeterred by complaints.
6. The fanatical worship of athletes.
7. By focusing their efforts on physical control and self-righteousness, generally bypassing the pursuit of spiritual integrity.
8. They enforce practices outside of Christ's finished work for spiritual redemption (e.g. Jehovah's Witnesses, Mormons, Roman Catholics...). The righteousness, power, and triumph of Christ is disgraced as a result.
9. When we are honest before God, we will acknowledge our many shortcomings and general frailty.

10. Many answers could be suggested (e.g. universal mass exhibits an awesome amount of power hinting at an omnipotent Creator).
11. Nature revealed nothing because it was fluid, featureless, and unlit (the universe was a deep sea of fluid materials with no light).
12. He made light a priority, implying that He likes revealing things.
13. Perhaps a fully-dimensional image of the completed universe.
14. The universe was stretched out at immense velocities, and time frames throughout the universe were dilated as a result.
15. Great amounts of energy are represented by even a little mass (that mass converts to energy by a factor of the speed of light squared).
16. Yes.
17. String theory.
18. Brian Greene, a secular physicist.
19. Richard Dawkins, a biologist and zealous advocate of Darwinism.
20. A sharply conscious Designer and Keeper.
21. They think that their Creator does not keep clear records, and that their own nature can satisfy God's standards (they degrade God).
22. Because they are "going about to establish their own righteousness" (as seen in Romans 10:1-3).
23. Sir Isaac Newton.
24. He was convinced by the orderliness and precision of nature of his need for a Savior.

THE RELEVANCE OF THE SETTING:
1. Because spiritual confidence is so deeply confirmed and final that secular logic is a clear waste of time and energy in comparison.
2. Because we cannot learn spiritual truth until we come to terms with spiritual facts, beginning with our gifted and guilty condition.
3. Because there is too much light near us and it blinds us to almost everything out there in space (illustrating the blindness caused by pride).
4. Our attention.
5. He designed nature to do His pleasure, so it is illogical to pursue a full understanding of nature without respect to Him (see Revelation 4:11).

6. People have often "loved darkness rather than light" simply "because their deeds were evil" (we are frankly bad by nature, see John 3:19).
7. When wrongs are tolerated on a personal level they will inevitably affect the professional level.
8. Sin is absolutely wrong, and provides legal grounds for absolute judgment.
9. The crucifixion of Jesus Christ.
10. The price for our sins had been paid; all the work that we could not do had been done for us—like money in the bank ready for withdrawal.
11. The Bible teaches us about the substitutionary death of Christ and our need of it. Believing the Bible means putting confidence in God's righteousness and recognizing the inadequacy of our own righteousness.
12. It is received by request in a spoken prayer to God at a definite time and place (like making an important phone call). You recognize the evil of your sins and your need of a Savior—that Christ's death was needed for you personally—and accept what He has victoriously done for you.

NOTES

CHAPTER 1
1. Friedrich Nietzsche, *The AntiChrist*, Section 47, quoted in Walter Kaufman, *The Portable Nietzsche* (New York: Viking, 1968), 627.
2. Brian Greene, *The Fabric of the Cosmos: Space, Time. And the Texture of Reality* (New York: Random House, Inc., 2004), 174.
3. Richard Dawkins, *The Blind Watchmaker: Why the evidence of evolution reveals a universe without design* (New York: W.W. Norton & Company, 1996), 147.
4. Massimo Pigliucci, *Denying Evolution: Creationism, Scientism, and the Nature of Science* (Sunderland, Mass.: Sinauer Associates, Inc.: 2002), 148.
5. Hal Lindsey, *The Late Great Planet Earth* (Grand Rapids, Mich.: Zondervan Publishing House, 1979), 26.
6. Charles Darwin, *The Origin of a Species* (1872; reissue, New York: Bantam Classics, 1999), 275.
7. Norman L. Geisler, *I Don't Have Enough Faith to Be an Atheist* (Wheaton, Ill.: Crossway Books, 2004), 152.
8. Dawkins, 225.
9. Ernst Mayr, *What Evolution Is* (New York: Basic Books, 2001), 209.
10. Ibid., 59.
11. Carl Zimmer, *Evolution: The triumph of an idea* (New York: HarperCollins Publishers Inc., 2006), 90.
12. Ibid., 91.
13. "Coelacanths," <http://www.aquaticcommunity.com/mix/coelacanths.php> (accessed 6 January 2012).
14. "Coelacanth," <http://www.sciencedaily.com/releases/2008/02/08> (accessed 7 January 2012).
15. Zimmer, 66.
16. Mayr, 47.
17. Dawkins, 246.
18. Ibid., 178.
19. Douglas J. Futuyma, *Evolution,* 2d ed. (Sunderland, MA: Sinauer Associates, Inc., 2009), 2.
20. Pigliucci, 73.
21. Sam Harris, *The Moral Landscape: How Science Can Determine Human Values* (New York, NY: Free Press, 2010), 72.
22. Greene, 173.
23. Ibid., 272.
24. Mayr, 174.
25. Ibid., 42.

26. Greene, 426.
27. Galileo, Letter to the Grand Duchess Christina (1615), quoted by C. Hummel, *The Galileo Connection: Resolving Conflicts between Science and the Bible* (Inter-Varsity Press, 1986), 106.

    Isaac Newton, *Newton's Principia. The mathematical principles of natural philosophy,* trans. Andrew Motte (New York: 1848), 544.

    William Paley, *Natural Theology: or, Evidences of the Existence and Attributes of the Deity, Collected from the Appearances of Nature* (1803; reprint: Cambridge University Press, 2009), 3-4.

    Gene Adair, *George Washington Carver* (New York: Chelsea House Publications, 1990), 80.

    E. Salaman, "A Talk With Einstein," *The Listener* 54 (1955), 370-371, quoted in *Jammer*, 123.

    Francis Collins, *The Language of God: A Scientist Presents Evidence for Belief* (New York: Free Press, 2006), 211.

    Lewis Campbell & William Garnet, *The Life of James Clerk Maxwell* (London: MacMillan and Co., 1882), 312.

    Henry Bence Jones, *The life and letters of Faraday,* Volume II (1870), 471.

    Kelvin, "Annual Address," speech given at the Christian Evidence Society, May 23, 1889.
28. Dawkins, 116.
29. Michael J. Behe, *Darwin's Black Box: The Biochemical Challenge To Evolution* (New York: Free Press, 2006), 41.
30. William A. Dembski, *The Design Revolution: Answering the Toughest Questions about Intelligent Design* (Downers Grove, Ill.: InterVarsity Press, 2004), 298.
31. Dawkins, 260.
32. Mae-Wan Ho and Peter T. Saunders (eds), *Beyond Neo-Darwinism: An Introduction to the New Evolutionary Paradigm* (London: Academic Press, 1984), 143-158.
33. Albrecht Fölsing, *Albert Einstein* (New York: Viking Press, 1997), 208-210.
34. Greene, 49.
35. Ibid., 139.

CHAPTER 2

1. Geisler, 181.
2. Harris, 28.
3. "Old Deluder Satan Act," *Records of the Governor and Company of the Massachusetts Bay in New England* (1853), II: 203, < http://www.constitution.org/primarysources/deluder.html>, (accessed 24 March 2012).
4. Dawkins, 241.

5. Lindsey, 31. (See *Appendix.*)
6. Mayr, 9.
7. Charles Darwin, *Autobiography* (Reprint, New York: Penguin Classics, 2002), 50.
8. Dawkins, 5.
9. Ibid, 37.
10. Mayr, 9.
11. Darwin, 50.
12. Harris, 96.
13. Ibid.
14. Ibid., 3.
15. Ibid.
16. Ibid., 97.
17. Ibid., 97-98.
18. Behe, 94.
19. Dembski, 216.
20. Behe, 88.
21. Harris, 103.
22. United States v. Grayson, 438 U.S. 41. Third Circuit United States Court of Appeals. 1978.
23. Pigliucci, 22.
24. John Foxe [prepared by W. Grinton Berry], *Foxe's Book of Martyrs, an edition for the people* (Greenville, S.C.: Ambassador International, 2005), 50-51.
25. William Kilpatrick, *Why Johnny Can't Tell Right From Wrong: Moral Illiteracy and the Case for Character Education* (New York: Simon and Schustler, 1992), 117.
26. Pigliucci, 37.
27. "An Inspiring Testimony: from the Diary of Christopher Columbus," <endtimepilgrim.org/Columbus.htm> Translated from Christopher Columbus's diary by August J. Kling and published in *The Presbyterian Layman*, October 1971, (accessed January 28, 2012).
28. Pigliucci, 37-38.
29. Ibid., 32.
30. Mayr, 148.
31. Harris, 183.
32. Ibid., 179.
33. Pigliucci, 41.
34. Dawkins, 1.
35. Ibid., 2.
36. Ibid., 2-3.
37. Ibid., 3.
38. Ibid., 141-142.

39. Ibid., 145.
  [a] Dawkins says that "a billion billion planet-years...will do nicely!" He is referring to planets roughly the size of the earth. If we assume that there are a trillion events possible per second, per atom we can easily calculate the total events possible. (1 trillion events)×(10^{50} atoms)×(60)×(60)× (24)×(365)×(billion)×(billion)×(billion)
  = **3.2×10^{96} events possible**
  [b] Since playing cards are each unique, the probability of randomly shuffling a deck of these cards back into factory order can be found directly by calculating the factorial of the total number of cards: 52! = 8.06×10^{67}. To find the probability of randomly shuffling *two separate decks* of cards 52! is simply squared: $(52!)^2$
  = **6.5×10^{135} events (shufflings) expected.**
  By dividing these results [a/b] we find that the event of randomly shuffling two decks of cards back into factory order is still very unlikely given the number of events provided by Dawkin's reasoning.
  3.2×10^{96} events possible /6.5×10^{135} events expected $\approx 10^{-40}$.
  This means that randomly *shuffling two decks of 52 cards* back into factory order using the number of events provided by Dawkins reasoning would be almost impossible: one in ten thousand trillion trillion trillion.
40. Ibid., 116.
41. Using a conservative estimate of 208 million letters and assuming, for ease of calculation, an equal distribution of the 26 letter options, we can calculate the probability. In the following operations, the letter "m" will represent one million or 10^6.
  Total combinations/total degeneracy
  =208m!/$(8m!)^{26}$
  $\approx *(208m)^{208m}(e)^{-208m}/(8m)^{(8m)(26)}(e)^{(-8m)(26)}$ *Stirling's approx.
  $\approx *(10)^{(8.318)(208m)}(e)^{-208m}/(10)^{(6.903)(8m)(26)}(e)^{(-8m)(26)}$ *rounded logs
  = $(10)^{1730m}(e)^{-208m}/(10)^{1436m}(e)^{-208m}$
      = $10^{1730m-1436m}$
      = 10^{294m}

Physicist Chris Clarke notes regarding this calculation:
"It cannot be stressed enough the number of assumptions and simplifying approximations that were used to find a number that has an exponent that is over a hundred million. This number demonstrates two very important things. First, it demonstrates that if something as basic as the letters in an encyclopedia have this many possible combinations how many more possible combinations must a complex entity like a cell have to actually work correctly, let alone routinely reproduce itself millions of times. Second, this demonstrates what has already been said, that life is a supernatural quality and that those who say otherwise are extremely disrespectful of both their Creator and the miracle that is life itself."

42. [a] (100 trillion events)×(10^{85}atoms)×(60)×(60)× (24)×(365)×(trillion^{60} years)×($10^{293,000,000}$universes)
 = $3.2×10^{293,000,826}$ events possible
 [b] $10^{294,000,000}$ events expected
 [a/b] $3.2×10^{293,000,826}/10^{294,000,000}$ = $3.2×10^{-999174}$
43. Kilpatrick, 28.
44. Harris, 64.
45. Ibid., 17.
46. Ibid., 33.
47. Ibid., 25.
48. Greene, 157.
49. Lindsey, 75.
50. William Grady, *What Hath God Wrought* (Knoxville, Tenn.: Grady Publications, 1996).
51. Dawkins, 193.
52. Mayr, 259.
53. J. Moll, R. de Oliveira-Souza, & R. Zahn, "The neural basis of moral cognition: sentiments, concepts, and values," *Ann NY Acad Sci, 1124* (2008): 162.
54. Harris, 33.
55. Geisler, 234.
56. Noah Webster, *American Dictionary of the English Language* (New York: S. Converse, 1828).
57. Brittany Olivarez, "Erik Erikson: Theory of Personality Development," 18 September 2009, <http://helpingpsychology.com/theory-of-personality-development-erik-erikson-model> (accessed 9 February 2012).
58. Adolf Hitler, *Mein Kampf Volume 1*, Chapter II "Race and People" (Zhingoora Books, 1941), 248.
59. Dawkins, 316.
60. Ibid., xiv.
61. Ibid., 230.
62. Richard Dawkins, *A Devil's Chaplin* (London: Weidenfeld & Nicolson, 2003), 121.
63. *The KJV Study Bible: Containing the Old and New Testaments with Study Notes from the QuickNotes Simplified Bible Commentary Series* (Uhrichsville, OH: Barbour Publishing, Inc., 2011), 115.
64. G. A. Riplinger, *In Awe of Thy Word: Understanding the King James Bible, Its Mystery and History, Letter by Letter* (Aravat, VA: AV Publications, 2003).
65. Arthur Westcott, *The Life and Letters of Brook Foss Westcott* and Arthur Hort, *The Life and Letters of Fenton John Anthony Hort*, < http://www.chick.com/reading/books/157/157_08b.asp> (accessed 02-13-2012).

66. Harris, 36.
67. Ibid., 130.
68. Pigliucci, 45-46.
69. Geisler, 279.
70. Harris, 124.

CHAPTER 3

1. Greene, 132.
2. Ibid., 133.
3. Rudolf Carnap, "Autobiography," in *The Philosophy of Rudolph Carnap*, ed. P. A. Schilpp (Chicago: Library of Living Philosophers, 1963), 37.
4. Greene, 144-145.
5. Noah Webster, *American Dictionary of the English Language* (New York: S. Converse, 1828).
6. Greene, 11.
7. Ibid., 122.
8. Samuel McCleod, "Jean Piaget," 2009, <http://www.simplypsychology.org/piaget.html> (accessed 13 February 2012).
9. Ibid.
10. Harris, 115.
11. Ibid., 121.
12. Ibid., 6.
13. Greene, 44.
14. Futuyma, 2.
15. Mayr, 117.
16. Zimmer, 95.
17. Mayr, 149.
18. Dawkins, *Watchmaker*, 37.
19. "Gregor Mendel," *Encyclopædia Britannica. Encyclopædia Britannica Online*. Encyclopædia Britannica Inc., 2012, <http://www.britannica.com/EBchecked/topic/374739/Gregor-Mendel> (accessed 18 March 2012).
20. Mayr, 150.
21. Ibid.
22. Ian Taylor, *In the Minds of Men* (Toronto: TFE Publishing, 1984) 126.
23. Dawkins, *Watchmaker*, 247.
24. "Monarchs," <http://butterflywebsite.com/Articles/uminn/monarchs.html> (accessed 20 February 2012).
25. "Monarch Life Span," < http://www.monarch-butterfly.com/life-span.html> (accessed 20 February 2012).
26. "Suicide Statistics," <http://www.cdc.gov/nchs/fastats/suicide.htm> (accessed 3 April 2019).
27. Harris, 181-182.

28. P. Slovic, "If I look at the mass I will never act": Psychic numbering and genocide, *Judgment and Decision Making, 2(2),* (2007): 79-95.
29. "Rabies," 10 February 2011, <http://www.ncbi.nlm.nih.gov/pubmedhealth/PMH0002310/> (accessed 23 February 2012).
30. "American Time Use Survey Summary," 22 June 2011, <http://www.bls.gov/news.release/atus.nr0.htm> (accessed 24 February 2012).
31. Pigliucci, 100.
32. Harris, 184.
33. Ibid., 46.
34. Dennis Corle, *Excuses for Conformity to the World* (Claysburg, Pa.: Revival Fires! Publishing, 2014), 3-4.
35. Futuyma, 10.
36. Mayr, 106.
37. James Nickel, *Mathematics: Is God Silent?* (Vallecito, California: Ross House Books, 2001), 184.
38. Dawkins, *Watchmaker,* 201.
39. Ibid., 296.

CHAPTER 4

1. "Sir Isaac Newton," *Encyclopedia Britannica. Encyclopedia Britannica Online.* Encyclopedia Britannica Inc., 2012, <http://www.britannica.com/EBchecked/topic/413189/Sir-Isaac-Newton> (27 February 2012).
2. Greene, 225.
3. Ibid.
4. Dawkins, *Watchmaker,* 55.
5. Charles Darwin, 186.
6. Francis Crick, *What Mad Pursuit: A Personal View of Scientific Discovery* (New York: BasicBooks, 1990), 138.
7. Dembski, 222.
8. Mayr, 147.
9. Greene, 157.
10. Ibid, 269-270.
11. Harris, 151.
12. Jonathan Wells, *Icons of Evolution: Science or Myth? Why Much of What We Teach About Evolution is Wrong* (Washington, D.C.: Regnery Publishing, Inc., 2000), 83.
13. Stephen Jay Gould, "Abscheulich! Atrocious!–The Precursor to the Theory of Natural Selection," *Natural History* (March, 2000), 42-49.
14. Henry Gee, *In Search of Deep Time: Beyond the Fossil Record to a New History of Life* (New York: The Free Press, 1999), 116-117.
15. Mayr, 174.
16. Ibid., 210.
17. Ibid., 13-14.
18. Ibid., 235.

19. Ibid., 235.
20. Dembski, 222.
21. Mayr, 239.
22. Dawkins, *Watchmaker,* 269.
23. Futuyma, 26.
24. Dawkins, *Watchmaker,* 274.
25. Zimmer, 108-109.
26. Mayr, 60.
27. Pigliucci, 73.
28. Harris, 36.
29. Futuyma, 165.
30. Zimmer, 81.
31. Futuyma, 2-3.
32. Ibid.
33. Wells, 178-187.
34. Ibid., 188.
35. Pigliucci, 194-195.
36. Harris, 158.
37. Ibid., 174.
38. Ibid., 159.

CHAPTER 5
1. "Martin Luther," <http://www.ndpsandiego.org/tiki-print.php?page=Resources> (accessed 12 March 2012).
2. Harris, 6.
3. Ibid., 16.
4. Ibid., 68.
5. Zimmer, 61.
6. Plastino, W.; Kaihola, L.; Bartolomei, P.; Bella, F. (2001), "Cosmic Background Reduction In The Radiocarbon Measurement By Scintillation Spectrometry At The Underground Laboratory Of Gran Sasso." *Radiocarbon* 43 (2A): 157–161.
7. "Bristlecone Pine," <http://www.blueplanetbiomes.org/bristlecone_pine.htm> (accessed 13 March 2012).
8. Dawkins, *Watchmaker,* 268-269.
9. Ibid., 233.
10. Ibid., 73.
11. Ibid.
12. Ibid., 181.
13. Ibid., 88.
14. Ibid., 90.
15. Mayr, 97.
16. Pigliucci, 151.
17. Harris, 166.

18. Lindsey, 132.
19. Harris, 183.
20. Mayr, 260.
21. Harris, 9.
22. Geisler, 295.
23. Robert Jastrow, *God and the Astronomer* (New York: Norton, 1978).
24. Greene, 354.
25. Ibid.
26. [a] Earth's solar *footprint* in miles = $\pi r^2 = \pi(4000)^2$
    = $\pi(4)^2(1000)^2 = 16\pi(million)$.
    [b] The surface area of the sphere where the circumference is defined by earth's orbit in miles = $4\pi r^2 = 4\pi(93 million)^2$
    = $4(93)^2\pi(million)^2 = 34,596\pi(million)^2$
    The ratio between these areas [a/b] shows approximately what portion of the solar radiation can be absorbed by the earth. This ratio [a/b] = $16\pi(million)/34,596\pi(million)^2 = .000462/million = 4.62(10)^{-10}$ which has a reciprocal of $(4.62(10)^{-10})^{-1} = 2,160,000,000$
    The earth absorbs approximately 1/2,160,000,000 of the energy that the sun emits. Which is a mass equivalent of
    4.3(million)(2200)(lbs.)/2,160,000,000 per second = 4.379 lbs. per second.
27. NYC is approximately 305mi^2; the earth's footprint is approximately $16\pi(million)$ miles^2. This means that the *most* (ignoring latitude) solar radiation that NYC could absorb is 305mi^2/$16\pi(million)$mi^2 = 1/164,804. The approximate mass equivalent of NYC sunlight energy per second = 4.379 lbs/160,000 =.0000274 lbs./sec. = .0000274 lbs.(60)(60)(12) /12 hours = 1.184 lbs./12 hours = 18.95 ounces/12 hours
28. "E=mc^2," <http://www.astronomycafe.net/qadir/q388.html> (accessed 17 March 2012).
    One gram is roughly equivalent to 3 Mw for a year [26,280 Mw hours]
    It can be drawn from this that since 1 ounce is roughly equivalent to 28.3495231grams, then 1 ounce is also roughly equivalent to (26,280 Mw hours)(28.3495231) of energy
    = approximately 745,025 Mw hours.
29. *Watts* during NYC strain
    = $(13,200)(1,000,000) = (1.32)(10)^{10}$watts
    Watt hours used at that level over a course of 48 hours
    – $(1.32)(10^{10})(60)(60)(48) = (2.28)(10)^{15}$watts
    wattsx10^7 = ergs
    2.28x10^{15}x10^7 = 2.28x10^{22}ergs
    To convert watts into grams divide the erg equivalent by c^2 where c is in centimeters.
    c^2 = (300,000km)^2 = (30,000,000,000cm)^2 = 9x10^{20}cm^2.

$2.28 \times 10^{22} / 9 \times 10^{20} = 25$ grams $= .88$ oz.

30. "New York City Power Demand,"
    <www.gsa.gov/graphics/regions/NYC_PlaNYC_508.ppt>
    NYC averages 50 million MWH/year
31. Average Mw hours used per hour in NYC
    $= 50$ million$/(365)(24) = 5708$ Mw hours per hour
    Mw hours per ounce/average Mw hours used by NYC
    $= 700,000/5708$
    $=122.6$ hours per ounce
    $= 61.3$ hours per half ounce…"toothbrush."
32. Greene, 354.
33. Greene, 347.
34. Ibid., 367.
35. Zimmer, 33.
36. Dawkins, *Watchmaker*, xvi.
37. Ibid., *Watchmaker*, xvi.
38. Pigliucci, 148.
39. D. Brewster, *Memoirs of Newton Volume 2, Chapter 27* (1855).

BIBLIOGRAPHY

Adair, Gene. *George Washington Carver.* New York: Chelsea House Publications, 1990.

Allister E. McGrath and Joanna Collicutt McGrath. *The Dawkins Delusion: Atheist Fundamentalism and the Denial of the Divine.* Downers Grove, Ill.: InterVarsity Press, 2007.

―――― E. McGrath. *Dawkins' God: Genes, Memes, and the Meaning of Life.* Malden, Mass.: Blackwell Publishing, 2005.

"American Time Use Survey Summary." 22 June 2011. <http://www.bls.gov/news.release/atus.nr0.htm> (accessed 24 February 2012).

"An Inspiring Testimony: from the Diary of Christopher Columbus." <endtimepilgrim.org/Columbus.htm> Translated from Christopher Columbus's diary by August J. Kling and published in *The Presbyterian Layman*, October 1971. (accessed January 28, 2012).

Behe, Michael J. *Darwin's Black Box: The Biochemical Challenge to Evolution.* New York: Free Press, 2006.

Brewster, D. *Memoirs of Newton, Volume 2.* 1855.

"Bristlecone Pine." <http://www.blueplanetbiomes.org/bristlecone_pine.htm> (accessed 13 March 2012).

Campbell, Lewis & William Garnet. *The Life of James Clerk Maxwell.* London: MacMillan and Co., 1882.

Carnap, Rudolph. "Autobiography," in *The Philosophy of Rudolph Carnap.* Edited by P. A. Schilpp. Chicago: Library of Living Philosophers, 1963.

"Coelacanth." <http://www.sciencedaily.com/releases/2008/02/08> (accessed 7 January 2012).

"Coelacanths." <http://www.aquaticcommunity.com/mix/coelacanths.php> (accessed 6 January 2012).

Collins, Francis. *The Language of God: A Scientist Presents Evidence for Belief.* New York: Free Press, 2006.

Corle, Dennis. *Excuses for Conformity to the World.* Claysburg, Pa.: Revival Fires! Publishing, 2014.

Corle, Dennis, *Humanism, The Religion of Public Education.* Claysburg, Pa.: Revival Fires! Publishing, 2013.

Crick, Francis. *What Mad Pursuit: A Personal View of Scientific Discovery.* New York: BasicBooks, 1990.

Darwin, Charles. *Autobiography.* Reprint; New York: Penguin Classics, 2002.

———, Charles. *The Origin of a Species*. 1872 Reissue, New York: Bantam Classics, 1999), 275.
Dawkins, Richard. *A Devil's Chaplin*. London: Weidenfeld & Nicolson, 2003.
———, Richard. *The Blind Watchmaker: Why the evidence of evolution reveals a universe without design*. New York: W.W. Norton & Company, 1996.
Dembski, William A. *The Design Revolution: Answering the Toughest Questions about Intelligent Design*. (Downers Grove, Ill.: InterVarsity Press, 2004), 298.
"$E=mc^2$." <http://www.astronomycafe.net/qadir/q388.html> (accessed 17 March 2012).
Fölsing, Albrecht. *Albert Einstein*. New York: Viking Press, 1997.
Foxe, John [prepared by W. Grinton Berry]. *Foxe's Book of Martyrs, an edition for the people*. Greenville, S.C.: Ambassador International, 2005.
Futuyma, Douglas J. *Evolution*. 2d ed. Sunderland, MA: Sinauer Associates, Inc., 2009.
Galileo, Letter to the Grand Duchess Christina (1615), quoted by C. Hummel, *The Galileo Connection: Resolving Conflicts between Science and the Bible* (Inter-Varsity Press, 1986), 106.
Gee, Henry. *In Search of Deep Time: Beyond the Fossil Record to a New History of Life*. New York: The Free Press, 1999.
Geisler, Norman L. *I Don't Have Enough Faith to Be an Atheist*. Wheaton, Ill.: Crossway Books, 2004.
Grady, William. *What Hath God Wrought!* Knoxville, Tenn.: Grady Publications, 1996.
Greene, Brian. *The Fabric of the Cosmos: Space, Time. And the Texture of Reality*. New York: Random House, Inc., 2004.
"Gregor Mendel," *Encyclopædia Britannica. Encyclopædia Britannica Online*. Encyclopædia Britannica Inc., 2012. <http://www.britannica.com/EBchecked/topic/374739/Gregor-Mendel> (accessed 18 March 2012).
Harris, Sam. *The Moral Landscape: How Science Can Determine Human Values*. New York, NY: Free Press, 2010.
Hitler, Adolf, *Mein Kampf Volume 1*, Chapter II "Race and People." Zhingoora Books, 1941.
Ho, Mae-Wan and Peter Saunders (eds). *Beyond Neo-Darwinism: An Introduction to the New Evolutionary Paradigm*. London: Academic Press, 1984.
Jastrow, Robert. *God and the Astronomer*. New York: Norton, 1978.
Jones, Henry Bence. *The life and letters of Faraday, Volume II*. 1870.
Kelvin. "Annual Address," speech given at the Christian Evidence Society. May 23, 1889.

Kilpatrick, William. *Why Johnny Can't Tell Right From Wrong: Moral Illiteracy and the Case for Character Education.* New York: Simon and Schuster, 1992.

The KJV Study Bible: Containing the Old and New Testaments with Study Notes from the QuickNotes Simplified Bible Commentary Series. Uhrichsville, OH: Barbour Publishing, Inc., 2011.

Lindsey, Hal. *The Late Great Planet Earth.* Grand Rapids, Mich.: Zondervan Publishing House, 1979.

"Martin Luther." <http://www.ndpsandiego.org/tiki-print.php?page=Resources> (accessed 12 March 2012).

Mayr, Ernst. *What Evolution Is.* New York: Basic Books, 2001.

McLeod, Samuel. "Jean Piaget." 2009. <http://www.simplypsychology.org/piaget.html> (accessed 13 February 2012).

Moll, J., R. de Oliveira-Souza, & R. Zahn, "The neural basis of moral cognition: sentiments, concepts, and values." *Ann NY Acad Sci, 1124* (2008): 161-180.

"Monarch Life Span." < http://www.monarch-butterfly.com/life-span.html> (accessed 20 February 2012).

"Monarchs." <http://butterflywebsite.com/Articles/uminn/monarchs.html> (accessed 20 February 2012).

"New York City Power Demand." <www.gsa.gov/graphics/regions/NYC_PlaNYC_508.ppt>.

Newton, Isaac. *Newton's Principia. The mathematical principles of natural philosophy,* trans. Andrew Motte. New York: 184.

Nickel, James. Mathematics: Is God Silent? Vallecito, California: Ross House Books, 2001.

Nietzsche, Friedrich. *The AntiChrist,* Section 47. Quoted in Walter Kaufman, *The Portable Nietzsche.* New York: Viking, 1968.

"Old Deluder Satan Act," *Records of the Governor and Company of the Massachusetts Bay in New England* (1853), II: 203, < http://www.constitution.org/primarysources/deluder.html> (accessed 24 March 2012).

Olivarez, Brittany. "Erik Erikson: Theory of Personality Development." 18 September 2009. <http://helpingpsychology.com/theory-of-personality-development-erik-erikson-model> (accessed 9 February 2012).

Paley, William. *Natural Theology: or, Evidences of the Existence and Attributes of the Deity, Collected from the Appearances of Nature.* 1803; reprint: Cambridge University Press, 2009.

Pigliucci, Massimo. *Denying Evolution: Creationism, Scientism, and the Nature of Science.* Sunderland, Mass.: Sinauer Associates, Inc., 2002.

"Rabies." 10 February 2011.
    <http://www.ncbi.nlm.nih.gov/pubmedhealth/PMH0002310/>
    (accessed 23 February 2012).

Riplinger, G. A. *In Awe of Thy Word: Understanding the King James Bible, Its Mystery and History, Letter by Letter.* Aravat, VA: AV Publications, 2003.

Salaman, E. "A Talk With Einstein." *The Listener* 54 (1955), 370-371, quoted in *Jammer*.

"Sir Isaac Newton." *Encyclopædia Britannica. Encyclopædia Britannica Online.* Encyclopædia Britannica Inc., 2012.
    <http://www.britannica.com/EBchecked/topic/413189/Sir-Isaac-Newton> (27 February 2012).

Slovic, P. "If I look at the mass I will never act": Psychic numbering and genocide, *Judgment and Decision Making, 2(2).* 2007.

Stephen Jay Gould. "Abscheulich! Atrocious!–The Precursor to the Theory of Natural Selection." *Natural History* (March, 2000).

"Suicide Statistics," <http://www.cdc.gov/nchs/fastats/suicide.htm> (accessed 22 February 2012).

Taylor, Ian. *In the Minds of Men.* Toronto: TFE Publishing, 1984.

United States v. Grayson, 438 U.S. 41. Third Circuit United States Court of Appeals. 1978.

Webster, Noah. *American Dictionary of the English Language.* New York: S. Converse, 1828.

Wells, Jonathan. *Icons of Evolution: Science or Myth? Why Much of What We Teach about Evolution is Wrong.* Washington, D.C.: Regnery Publishing, Inc., 2000.

Westcott, Arthur. *The Life and Letters of Brook Foss Westcott;* Arthur Hort. *The Life and Letters of Fenton John Anthony Hort.* < http://www.chick.com/reading/books/157/157_08b.asp> (accessed 02-13-2012).

Zimmer, Carl. *Evolution: The triumph of an idea.* New York: HarperCollins Publishers Inc., 2006.

CREDITS

"Tree of Life" from Ernst Haeckel's *The Evolution of Man* (Published 1879).

"DNA" from National Institutes of Health, "Talking Glossary of Genetic Terms," National Human Genome Research Institute. <http://www.genome.gov/glossary/?id=48> (accessed 31 March 2012).

Adaptation of "Punnett Square," Pbroks13 (2008), used under a Creative Commons Attribution-ShareAlike license: http://creativecommons.org/licenses/by-sa/3.0/. This adaptation is licensed under the same Creative Commons Attribution-ShareAlike license: http://creativecommons.org/licenses/by-sa/3.0/.

"Radiocarbon dating calibration" Stuiver, M., P. J. Reimer and T. F. Braziunas. High-Precision Radiocarbon Age Calibration for Terrestrial and Marine Samples. Radiocarbon 40, 1127-1151 (1998). Downloadable from University of Washington, Quaternary Isotope Lab: http://depts.washington.edu/qil/datasets/uwten98_14c.txt

INDEX

abiogenesis, 22
abortion, 43
adaptations, 103
afterlife, 63
America, 11-13, 35-36, 110
antibiotics, 139
anxiety, 41-42
apathy, 81
apes, 133-134
astrophysics, 19
atheism, 53
atoms, 24
authority, 48, 84
bacteria, 139
beginning, 19, 166
Behe, Michael, 24
belief, 53, 95
Berlin, 74
Bible, 80-82
biology, 18, 137
blood, 44
blue–green algae, 16
bristlecone pine, 152
Buddhism, 53
bulldog, 166
butterflies, 176
calculus, 176
Cambrian, 12-13
Carnap, Rudolf, 91
cells, 24, 57, 117
Chaloner, 130
children, 39-41, 64
Christ, 175
Christianity, 164
cichlids, 14
classification, 25, 164
coelacanth, 15-16
Collins, Francis, 177
Columbus, 51
combinations, 104
compassion, 109-110
conscience, 62
consciousness, 174
consequentialism, 19, 61
consistency, 16, 65
conviction, 142
cosmos, 179
counterfeit, 48, 73
Courtenay-Latimer, Marjorie, 15
Creator, 50, 62, 167
Crick, Francis, 127
crime, 39
critics, 80
cyanobacteria, 16
cynics, 66
Darwin, Charles, 12
dating, carbon, 150
Dawkins, Richard, 10
decay, 9, 55, 150
deception, 38, 130
defensiveness, 83
Dembski, William, 24
depreciation, 47
depression, 108
detention, 40
dignity, 72
disciples, 16
discipline, 40
disease, 42, 184
diversity, 13-17, 132
$E=mc^2$, 170
education, 11, 35
Einstein, Albert, 28, 91, 95
embryos, 131
Encyclopedia Britannica, 24, 60
energy, 23, 170
entertainment, 112
entropy, 19, 65
equilibrium, 152
Erikson, Erik, 75
evil, 12, 39
evolution, 27, 37, 44, 137
    theory of, 12
    Darwinism, 54, 137

extinct, 15, 133
eyes, 125
faith, 89
fiction, 112
fortune, 54
fossils, 12, 16, 132
friends, 161
Futuyma, Douglas, 18
galaxies, 170
gay, 163
Gee, Henry, 132
Geisler, Norman, 34
spontaneous generation, 22, 60
genes, 25, 102
   recombination of, 116
geocentricity, 51
Grady, 66
Greene, Brian, 9
Haeckel, Ernst, 131
half–life, 150
happiness, 162
Harris, Sam, 19
hereditary traits, 115
Higgs field, 128
Hindu, 175
Hitler, Adolf, 76, 153
Holocaust, 80
Holy Spirit, 95
hominids, 134
hope, 34, 141, 181
Hort, Fenton, 80
humanism, 59
humility, 75, 83
hydrophobia, 111
ingratitude, 47
intermediates, 132, 157
Islam, 165
Israel, 11, 36, 66
kindness, 70-71
law, 108, 124
life, 70
light years, 171-172
Lindsey, Hal, 12
links, 12, 132-134

Linnaeus, Carolus, 25
literal, 25
logic, 162
love, 34
Luther, Martin, 146
Maker, 158
mass, 169
matter, 23, 170
Mayr, Ernst, 13
Mein Kampf, 76
Mendel, Gregor, 101
Messiah, 36
Middle Ages, 48
Milky Way, 51
minimum complexity, 14
missionaries, 110
Mohammed, 165
monarch butterfly, 106
morality, 20, 150, 180
motivation, 71
movies, 111
mutation, 14, 44, 156
natural selection, 99, 121, 155
   utility of, 14, 156
nature, 9, 53
Nazi, 80
Nelson, Gareth, 27
neuroimaging, 42
Newton, Isaac, 123, 178
Nietzsche, Friedrich, 8
Old Deluder Satan Act, 35
ontogeny, 131
order, 9, 105
origins, 22
orthodox Jews, 36
Oyamel forest, 107
pain, 95
parsimony, 135
passwords, 126
penicillin, 139
phantasms, 90
phenotype, 160
photons, 57
physics, 59

Piaget, Jean, 93
Pigliucci, Massimo, 9
Podolsky, 92
polygenes, 117
pornography, 39
predators, 158
prediction, 11
pressures, 15
pride, 74
progression, 12, 17, 128
proof, 21
prophesy, 36
psychology, 18
psychopaths, 41
punishment, 40
Punnett square, 102
quantum mechanics, 92
rabies, 111
races, 132, 138
radiocarbon, 152
recessive traits, 101
Redeemer, 162, 181
relativity, 28
religions, 164, 174
resemblances, 135
responsibility, 9, 36
Riplinger, Gail, 80
ruler, 179
salvation, 182
Satan, 50
Savior, 155, 161, 177
schemas, 93
Scripture, 80
selfishness, 67
self-respect, 75
Shinto, 175
similarity, 133-34
simple, 183
sin, 37, 55, 180
skeletons, 13
skepticism, 21
soul, 48, 173
spacetime, 29, 97
species, 105, 132

spiritual, 35, 53, 161
stars, 59
storytelling, 38, 78
strata, 133
string theory, 172
suicide, 108
Supreme Court, 46
survival, 68, 99, 126
Sword, 107
symmetry, 124
television, 110
textual criticism, 79
theologians, 77
thermodynamics
   first law of, 23
   second law of, 128
time, 28, 169
timeframes, 169
tolerance, 34
tongues, 35
traits, 100
transgressions, 42
translation, 80
tree of life, 27
trust, 93
truth, 19, 33, 48, 54
unbelief, 79, 111
ungodliness, 84
universe, 9, 32, 58
variation, 14, 101, 105, 116
versions, 81
Lake Victoria, 14
Webster, Noah, 75
well-being, 72, 161, 164
Wells, Jonathan, 140
Westcott, Brooke, 80
will, 45, 141
worldview, 61, 64
Zimmer, Carl, 14

www.ingramcontent.com/pod-product-compliance
Lightning Source LLC
Chambersburg PA
CBHW050630300426
44112CB00012B/1738